The
Beginning
Comes
After
the
End

Also Available from Haymarket Books by Rebecca Solnit

The Beginning Comes After the End

Notes on a World of Change

Rebecca Solnit

Haymarket Books
Chicago, Illinois

Published in 2026 by
Haymarket Books
P.O. Box 180165
Chicago, IL 60618
773-583-7884
www.haymarketbooks.org
info@haymarketbooks.org

ISBN: 979-8-88890-451-0

Distributed to the trade in the US through Consortium Book Sales
and Distribution (www.cbsd.com) and internationally through Ingram
Publisher Services International (www.ingramcontent.com).

This book was published with the generous support of Lannan
Foundation, Wallace Action Fund, and Marguerite Casey Foundation.

Special discounts are available for bulk purchases by organizations and
institutions. Please email info@haymarketbooks.org for more information.

Cover design by Abby Weintraub.

Library of Congress Cataloging-in-Publication data is available.

Printed in Canada by union labor. Library of Congress Control
Number: 2025948101

10 9 8 7 6 5 4 3 2 1

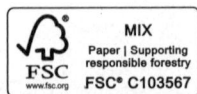

"We are caught in an inescapable network of mutuality, tied in a single garment of destiny. Whatever affects one directly, affects all indirectly."

—Martin Luther King Jr.

"We are living through a revolt against the future. The future will prevail."

—Anand Giridharadas

"We're the ancestors of tomorrow, so we behave accordingly."

—Madonna Thunder Hawk

Contents

Swimming Upstream

The hilltop overlooking the ocean did not look like the place where "hope and history rhyme," where an old prophecy would be declared to have come true, where the long arc of history had bent toward justice. On that morning of October 17, 2024, about three dozen of us stood where last year's green grass, after turning gold at the end of the rainy season, had faded to a dull tan during California's long dry season. The earth looked parched. To the north of us, the hills sloped steeply downhill into a creek that, as it reached the ocean, turned into an estuary, a tidal zone where fresh and saltwater meet. To the east of us, farmland and pastureland spread for miles. A strong steady wind came from the Pacific, clearing the air and making it hard to hear people speak, but they spoke.

We stood about sixty miles north of San Francisco on 466 acres of ranchland that had been in the hands of white people since the nineteenth century, newly purchased by the Western Rivers Conservancy and handed back to the Federated Indians of Graton Rancheria to care for in perpetuity, and Graton tribal members were present. This place rising from the south bank of San Antonio Estero was one of many sites of land-back that year—the return of land in North America to its original stewards. Environmental organizations and government departments tasked with land management had, in recent years, begun to recognize that Indigenous stewardship and leadership were among the best ways to restore and protect the land. Indigenous groups had long advocated for that protection and the restoration of their rights.

Also that October of 2024, a few hundred miles north along the California coast, the biggest dam removal in US history had just been completed, the result of decades of campaigning by local tribes and other supporters of a free-flowing river. Four dams had come down on the 263-mile-long Klamath River. The land that emerged from the stagnant waters behind the dams is being restored and replanted with thousands of young trees and literal tons of native-plant seeds by tribal governments that live up and down this great salmon river that had been choked and stifled for more than a century. Chinook salmon, stopped for that dammed century from completing their journeys to their ancient spawning grounds, had surged upstream almost immediately. The day before we gathered on that hilltop, the first salmon in more than a century had swum the Klamath's sinuous route through northernmost California all the way to Oregon. "It's amazing," said Ron Reed, a fisherman from the Karuk tribe. "That's what we've prayed for," he told a newspaper.

Near where the Klamath meets the Pacific, another 125 acres purchased by the Save the Redwoods League had been handed back to the Yurok tribe earlier that year. The league had been founded in 1918 by eugenicists who saw preserving nature as aligned with preserving their kind of white elite against immigrants and others, and these and the League's other recent land-back projects (as well as published apologies) marked profound shifts in its values and worldview, reflecting those in the wider culture. In May 2025, the Western Rivers Conservancy completed the return to the Yurok of an additional 73 square miles of land—47,097 acres—on Blue

Creek, a major tributary of the Klamath River. Six days before we met at San Antonio Estero, three hundred miles south, the Chumash Heritage National Marine Sanctuary was established, protecting more than a hundred miles of coastline and more than four thousand square miles of the Pacific Ocean off that coast. The Northern Chumash Tribal Council had submitted the proposal to the federal government nine years earlier.

From Maine to Washington state, land seized generations before is coming back. Not all of it, not enough of it, but every acre signifies a shift. So much has to happen for any one of these returns to happen, so much had to change just to recognize the presence of Native Americans after decades of erasure and institutionalized forgetting, following upon centuries of genocide.* For more than thirty years, I had watched as Native Americans and their supporters had, step by step, shifted what was possible and imaginable to reach this point. It was the end of something, the beginning of something else.

Other changes are happening. Up and down the Pacific Coast, local groups, including schools, are cleaning up salmon streams and watching the fish return and paying attention to these wild creatures and the systems they're part of, in ways most non-native inhabitants of the West Coast hadn't comprehended or cared about before. (The Pacific coast salmon population once numbered in the

---

* A week after that gathering at San Antonio Estero, President Joe Biden traveled to Arizona to apologize for the cultural and literal genocide committed by the government boarding schools in which Native children were forced to lose their language and culture, saying they "will always be a significant mark of shame, a blot on American history. For too long, this all happened with virtually no public attention, not written about in our history books, not taught in our schools." Eight years earlier, on December 5, 2016, at the Standing Rock camp in South Dakota resisting the Dakota Access pipeline, hundreds of veterans of the US military got down on their knees and apologized for the role of the military in murdering and displacing Native Americans. Lakota spiritual leader Leonard Crow Dog accepted the apology.

tens of millions, and they were before this decline a major food source for the region's Indigenous populations, as well as for wild-life.) They are perceiving and valuing the world around them in a new way and acting on that perception and those values. This de-votion to salmon was one example of a growing engagement with the natural and cultural histories of place across the continent—to recover what had been forgotten, tend what had been neglected, re-store what had been damaged. Of course, not everyone is on board, and conflicts can be intense between the protectors and the forces of exploitation and erasure, but it marks a profound shift, maybe a return to what had been forgotten, maybe the end of an era of institutionalized forgetting.

The beginning comes after the end. A chrysalis is the begin-ning of a butterfly, but in that chrysalis is no elegant transition. The caterpillar falls apart—it turns to goo, and something profound-ly different reconstitutes from it, guided by the hitherto dormant imaginal cells. In that slurry, the dissolving caterpillar's immune system perceives the imaginal cells as alien and attacks them. But they survive, multiply, and set in motion the instructions to become a butterfly. A many-legged crawler becomes a six-legged winged creature, an animal that devours leaves becomes one that sips nec-tar from flowers. In recent years, as we've paid closer attention to the natural world and learned more about it from scientists, this metamorphosis has become a metaphor for the transformation of society, often with the sense that we are at the stage of dissolution, imaginal cells under attack. A butterfly is the end of a caterpillar. The beginning—the next era—comes after the end of the last one, and in between comes a lot of falling apart.

There is a way to tell the story of who we were and where we were in that fall of 2024 in terms of electoral politics that is, to put it mildly, dismal and discouraging. But deeper currents of change are at work. This era is not one in which everything is fine and all ancient wrongs have been righted, but it is one in which important parts of a society, maybe a civilization, have changed profoundly, even while the right is trying to change them back. The most profound change is in worldview, when it comes to how settler-colonialists recognize and understand Indigenous presence and rights, and so many other foundational realities about our world, around gender, around race, around justice and equality, around nature itself and the science that explains it. The practical, tangible changes are consequences of these changed views.

Our world has changed more than almost anyone imagined, in ways both wonderful and terrible, often in ways no one anticipated, and the sheer profundity of change in the past guarantees that this change will continue, that stability is not an option, but participating in directing change might be, if we recognize it. That October morning in 2024, we stood on a hilltop, and we stood in a present that had once been an unimaginable future in the way it reconnected to a suppressed past. It had been reached step by step, as the poet Antonio Machado put it, on "a road made by walking."

There are many fragments to this mosaic of changes I want to chart, and underlying most of them is a shift toward the idea that everything is connected, that the world is a network of interrelated systems, that the isolated individual is at best a fiction, and that the natural and social realms run more on collaboration and cooperation than competition. It's a shift away from many of the old hierarchies and segregations and the cruelties they normalized. These ideas of interconnection emerge from many sources, from new economic models and new scientific ideas about biology and psychology, from Buddhist and Indigenous worldviews, from shifting values, from hopes and desires to undo the terrible loneliness and tendency toward isolation and the severing of connections and relationships between people, peoples, and people and nature, that seem entrenched in current social configurations. I believe we're also witnessing a shift from capitalism's tendency to see even the living, even humans, as dead things—as objects and commodities—to Indigenous and animist worldviews that regard being, sentience, and rights as qualities of rivers and mountains, as well as of plants and animals. Of course, the tricky part of that sentence is the "we": not everyone is on board, and the backlash is ferocious.

The ranch property where we gathered on that October day is shaped like a puzzle piece. The small town of Dillon Beach and a private development border its south side, and its north side is formed by the San Antonio Estero. If you generalized, you could say that the broad stream set between steep hills runs west to the Pacific, but it wanders between the steep hills in wide unhurried arcs. On the beach, the running water pools, as small estuaries do up and down the coast, forming an environment that is neither saltwater nor fresh. In that mixture lives an endangered fish the size of a child's finger, the northern tidewater goby, that only thrives in these in-between waters. Upstream from the goby live red-legged frogs, listed as threatened, one step less imperiled than endangered. On the hills where we stood that windy day lives the Myrtle's silverspot butterfly, which lays its eggs on the western dog violet. The violet's leaves form the first and only food of the caterpillars that hatch from those eggs; the butterfly drinks the nectar of native plants such as western pennyroyal, yellow sand verbena, seaside daisy, and mule ears. Listed as endangered, this small, speckled, golden-brown butterfly is only known to exist in this location and three others nearby. Somehow, these species had survived a century and a half of cattle ranching in this place.

The browning stems of the wild iris that blooms in early spring grew in scattered clusters across the hilltops and slopes. Deer browsed the hills that hawks soared over. When I joined the small group taking the sometimes precarious, eroded path down to the estuary and beach, I saw the waterline was crisscrossed with the tracks of raccoons foraging for what washed up at high tide. An osprey flew over us. Stone tools and other traces of longtime Coast Miwok presence had been found on the site by the archeologist who worked for the tribe.

Graton Rancheria chairman Greg Sarris, a tall man who looked younger than his seventy-two years, in jeans the color of the sky and a suede jacket the color of the grass, spoke to reporters and others gathered. I had known him a long time as a fellow writer, and we chatted a bit together. He saw the day as the fulfillment of the prophecy by the Kashaya Pomo Dreamer Essie Parrish in the 1950s, who urged her listeners to preserve the teachings of the old people, because "one day, the white people would come to us to learn how to take care of the land." The history that led to this moment twisted and turned like San Antonio Estero. The Federated Indians of Graton Rancheria is a Native nation formed of Coast Miwok and Southern Pomo people, who had traditionally inhabited the lands north of the Golden Gate Bridge now called Marin and Sonoma Counties.

The Native people of coastal California had been devastated by disease and the Spanish missions that spread up from what's now the Mexican border to Sonoma from 1769 to 1833. Far more destruction, including massacres, legalized slaughter, and enslavement, came after the United States claimed title to the land after the Mexican–American War of 1846–1848 and the Gold Rush began. When it came to signing treaties and receiving federal recognition as nations entitled to land and other rights, most Native Californians got little or nothing. The Coast Miwok who'd been coercively Christianized at Mission San Rafael became a landless people.

In 1922, the Miwok and Pomo peoples were given a fifteen-acre holding—a rancheria was the term used in California for these small collectively owned Native lands—in the hamlet of Graton in Sonoma County. While nineteenth-century genocide had often been bloodily violent, the twentieth-century version was blandly bureaucratic but just as bent on erasure of cultural identity and nation status. The US Congress passed the California Rancheria Act of 1958, declaring that forty-one rancherias—including the one at Graton—were no longer the shared possessions of California tribes, merely private property of individuals, and privatization was often a prelude to losing those lands altogether. Federal policy at that time aimed to assimilate Native people into mainstream society, to be achieved by destroying them as cultures and as communities in relationship to place.

Greg spoke that day of how one woman and her daughter held onto one acre of Graton Rancheria, and in the watershed year of 1992 reached out to him. With their urging, he helped write legislation that was signed into law by President Clinton in 2000, giving them back federal recognition with the benefits and powers that includes. The resultant group, which calls itself the Federated Indians of Graton Rancheria, now has 1,537 members, all descendants, he said that day, of fourteen women who survived the genocide and maintained what they could of their cultures. Thanks to partnership with the park service at Point Reyes National Seashore and other public land managers, the tribe now has jurisdiction over a hundred thousand acres.

Packed into that paragraph, the journey from one acre to a hundred thousand, official nonexistence to recognition seems simple and straightforward, but heaven and earth, law and culture, had to be moved, shaken, reimagined, dismantled, and rebuilt in order to arrive at that day. We live in a world utterly unlike the one Greg was born into in the 1950s and in which I arrived early in the 1960s, when Native Californians and Native Americans were largely written out of the histories and the Spanish missions were romanticized. Even our personal lives, mine as a woman, his as a gay man and Pomo / Coast Miwok / Filipino descendant, had taken forms unlikely or even impossible when we were growing up near here, he in Santa Rosa, about the same distance northeast of San Antonio Estero as Novato, where I grew up, was southeast of it.

These were tiny pieces of the big picture of change that means we in the 2020s live in a world that would be unbelievable and maybe inconceivable to people sixty or seventy years earlier. We inhabit and inherit a world that has changed bit by bit, in ways so vast and so varied, in so many spheres of everyday life, that the transformation has hardly been described.

2

Winged Seeds

Seeds spread by many means. Some, encased in fruit, are eaten by
birds and excreted on the wing far from the berry bush; some have
their own wings or are shaped like parachutes so they can travel on
the wind, as do the seeds of dandelions and maples; some explode
from the pod, as do the beanlike seeds of wisteria; some travel by
sticking to fur or hair or fabric; some are carried away and stored
by squirrels whose forgetfulness begets forests. Some seeds lie dormant for years or decades and only germinate when fire sweeps over
the land. Sequoias, those largest beings standing on the earth, only
drop their seeds when fire comes and melts the resin in the cones.
In destruction is their regeneration.

Ideas, too, have many ways of traveling, and some ideas that
begin in obscurity spread and proliferate and strengthen to become
powerful elements of a culture, a society, a civilization. The ideas
that have taken root in the last three quarters of a century have
borne fruit—as laws, rights, beliefs, roles, possibilities that did not
exist before—and they add up to changes so profound that they
amount to the end of a civilization and the beginning of another
with different values and beliefs. We often speak as though we are
here to toil, endlessly planting and cultivating seeds and seedlings,
but we have also feasted on harvests from what was sown and tended by those who came before.

You can chop down a tree, but ideas tend to outlive their attacks. You can, for example, take away rights but not belief in those rights; ideas in this sense are trees that will not become seeds again, are the genies in *The Arabian Nights* who, once released from captivity, will do anything but be bottled up again. Undoubtedly, some American women who lost reproductive rights after the June 24, 2022, decision overturning the *Roe v. Wade* Supreme Court decision forty-nine years earlier believe that they and others should not have those rights (though, often, people who don't believe in the general principle grant themselves an exemption or bury it all in cognitive dissonance or denial). They are significantly outnumbered by people who believe in those rights for all. The memory of rights taken away will not be uprooted easily, and while the US has increasingly allowed states to restrict those rights, other nations, including Mexico, Argentina, Ireland, and Spain (and some US states) have expanded them. In June 2025, the United Kingdom overturned an 1861 law criminalizing abortion, used mostly to punish women who had abortions after twenty-four weeks (and in 2019, decriminalized abortion in Northern Ireland).

Ideas have power, and while those who support them often dismiss that power, those who fear them recognize they can change the world. Environmentalist Gus Speth writes that visions of a better world "will not compete yet in today's practical politics" but calls them "the first blueprints of the future, the playing fields of radical hope, the dreams that stuff is made of." Ideas are seeds in that they are beginnings; if they succeed, they do so as they take on more tangible and concrete forms. They become how the world is, how we do things; they guide our practical actions, whether it's our relationships to each other or the land. Seeds—or imaginal cells, the instructions for transformation.

This is a long essay in the form of a short book about the pro-found changes of the past several decades, about those who planted and tended the seeds, about how ideas became actualities, how we came to live in a time so different from the past, how this year may look much like last year but 2025 looked nothing at all like 1965 and is wilder in many ways, good and bad, than anyone dreamed of back then. The good parts mostly came about because of cam-paigns, struggles, visions acted on, and the participants made it up as they went along, incorporating what they learned, redefining as they went, setting new goals when they reached earlier ones or course-correcting when they learned from their mistakes.

This is a reminder that you do not have to picture the destina-tion to reach it or at least draw closer to it, you just need to choose a direction and keep on walking—though that metaphor makes it sound as though it already exists, if at a distance, rather than that the process itself creates it and covers the distance between the idea and the actuality. You can arrive at a new social reality and its consequences, such as land-back or rights affirmed or legislation passed or equality established or access opened up. All of this can also be undone, and there is an immense backlash against what these decades have brought us, but the fury of that backlash is itself evidence of the significance of what was achieved.

This is not a book claiming that the work is finished or that we have arrived in an ideal anything or that all of us are on board. It's an exploration of transformation on an epic scale and in almost every avenue of life and thought. Like everything I write, it's not meant to be comprehensive—rather, think of it as a map on which you can fill in missing details and trace your own routes against mine or clarify your vision by disagreeing with mine. It's a book that reaches across many disciplines and topics, in none of which I am officially expert though I've spent many decades paying close attention to many of them. (I'd be aghast at my own audacity if I didn't think that someone needed to try to connect these dots across space, time, and topics, and that it's better to do it imperfectly than not to do it at all.) It's inevitably shaped by my vantage point, as a white woman on the left coast of North America, a witness to six decades of transformation, a writer with an enthusiasm for tracing patterns, a climate activist, a former Indigenous rights activist, a lover of street protests, a feminist, the granddaughter of refugees fleeing genocide in Eastern Europe on one side, the great-granddaughter of Irish Catholics fleeing British colonialism on the other.

There's a famous passage in the prison journals of the Italian Marxist philosopher Antonio Gramsci. He wrote, around 1930, "La crisi consiste appunto nel fatto che il vecchio muore e il nuovo non può nascere: in questo interregno si verificano i fenomeni morbosi più svariati." A more popular variant runs, "Il vecchio mondo sta morendo. Quello nuovo tarda a comparire. E in questo chiaroscuro nascono i mostri." My Italian friend Fiamma Montezemolo translated the latter version of this famous statement for me as, "The old world is dying. The new one is slow in appearing. In this light and shadow, monsters arise."

Gramsci wrote this almost a century ago, in Fascist Italy, about other deaths, other births, other monsters (or, in his original, morbid symptoms) than ours, but it still stands as a beautiful summary of what it's like to be in a world in crisis facing an uncertain future. He could not possibly mean by it what I mean by it, because many worlds have died and been born since he wrote it. And while many think of the world dying as something looming only in the future, Indigenous people of the Americas and others who've survived genocide and colonialism know that they live after the deaths of worlds.*

---

* *World* in my usage does not mean Earth: many parts of the biosphere are

British environmental writer Robert Macfarlane wrote to me, "Yes, the monsters are abroad, but as we know *monster* comes from *monstrare*, meaning to demonstrate and to warn. Monsters—the bad kind—show us the way forwards, as well as pushing us back." That the old world is dying is widely acknowledged and addressed. The old ways of doing things no longer fit who we have become: the systems fail, break, decay, fall into corruption; anachronistic school curriculums and journalistic and political norms, social roles and customs, rules, laws, and institutions don't offer us equipment to face the realities of our time, whether they feel like cages or outgrown garments or broken tools. Poverty and displacement, degradation and alienation are byproducts of voracious, ruthless systems committed to inequality and indifferent to human rights and the rights of nature, which is to say that they are violence by other means, and sometimes they are the violence itself.

Climate catastrophes, from melting glaciers and permafrost to catastrophic wildfires and floods, the abundance of garbage and abandoned goods, of toxic and nuclear waste and oil spills and mine tailings: they're evidence that a fossil-fuel economy and one based on disposability, overconsumption, and alienation ends up as destruction and waste. So many old orders are falling apart, so many systems no longer work, so many assumptions no longer fit. Cruelty, greed, and division are not new, but when the old order that institutionalized them is threatened, its beneficiaries come out fighting to hold onto advantages that used to go unquestioned.

Uncertainty is full of possibilities and not only positive ones. However flawed or ugly an existing system, it's reasonable to

---

badly damaged or destroyed, many species threatened, some have already become or will go extinct, but life on Earth most likely has billions of years yet to come. It means instead the systems and ideas and powers that organize the human realm or a part of it, so that the Chinese world of 2,500 years ago was not the Greek or Mayan world of that era.

wonder whether what succeeds it will be better or worse or terrifying, especially if that system serves you. In many cases, monsters arise out of the attachment to the dying order, monsters willing to use monstrous violence to prevent the new world from being born. You can imagine them as akin to the caterpillar's immune system attacking the imaginal cells that guide its transition into a butterfly, for Gramsci's famous sentence describes a sociopolitical condition much like what takes place in the chrysalis. Monsters take the forms of authoritarians, corporations bent on quarterly profits at the expense of the long-term fate of the earth; of racism, misogyny, and other inculcated hates that serve to divide, silence, and marginalize; of Silicon Valley's "move fast and break things" ethos that has broken much and threatens to break far more.

Silicon Valley's oligarchs are committed to harnessing their new technologies to that old and dying world of inequality and hierarchy, of extreme wealth and poverty, extreme power and powerlessness, of isolation and alienation, of extractivism and commodification even of children's imaginations and all our dreams. Many of its richest men countenance and even egg on the destruction of the world while seeking to shelter themselves and only themselves and their families from it. They believe devoutly in many kinds of isolationism, in ruthless exploitation and endless growth, in ideas that conflict with what we now understand about human nature and nature itself as the limits of the earth—which some of them, infatuated with postwar fantasies of colonizing space and other planets, want to leave. Our psyches are where they go strip-mining, but they savage the natural world, too.

The novelist turned climate thinker Amitav Ghosh has another take on the monsters, writing, "What is distinctive about our time is that its monsters consist not only of political extremists of all kinds, but also of weather events that could not have been conceived of in Gramsci's lifetime." He means, I believe, the unnatural nature of weather events due to human recklessness. Political actors are the fathers of these weather monsters in their selfishness, accepting the destruction of the common good for personal benefit, or for a grotesque version of such benefit. Rather than build a better world for all, they unleash desperation and chaos out of confidence in their ability to stand apart—in gated communities, luxury towers, armored cars, private islands, with the help of private police—from the common fate.

They believe they are not strangling a new world being born; they are rejuvenating a dying world, making it thrive again, or pretending it never declined. Donald Trump's slogan, "Make America Great Again," I always thought of as code for "Make America 1958 (or perhaps 1858) Again." Like all fascism, it promises to restore a lost majesty, a lost hierarchy—in this case, the tidiness of a rigidly hierarchical order in which men and women, whites and nonwhites, citizens and immigrants, rich and poor all assumed their assigned roles, in which mobility, fluidity, equality were banished, in which conformity as heterosexuality, female submission, and Christianity (the version of it at odds with Jesus's teachings) are all obligatory. Fascism claims the past, or a fantasy version of it, as paradise while it tries to strangle the future and insists that order only comes through repression and the reinstatement of inequalities.

But, in a phrase sometimes attributed to Pablo Neruda, "You can cut down the flowers, but you can't stop the spring." A new world is being born. In 1978, Thomas Berry wrote, in words echoing Gramsci's, "We are in trouble because we do not have a good story. We are in between stories. The Old Story—the account of how the world came to be and we fit into it—is not functioning properly and we have not learned the New Story." *We* is a problematic term even when it's a necessary one. I'd argue that we have many good stories, both old and new, almost half a century on from that declaration, not least because the contemporary *we* is at its best a broader constituency than the one Berry may have been thinking of when he wrote those sentences. Progressives have a habit of saying, "Tomorrow the good thing should begin," when, often, the good things are underway, even if embryonic, embattled, or otherwise uncertain.

That old story was shouted to drown out the other stories, and it insisted there was one story, the Eurocentric story, the colonial story, the Christian story, the patriarchal story, the top-down story, the story of conquest and domination as progress. That old story had at one time, centuries before, been an upstart story seeking to eclipse the previous versions. Much of the revolution of our era has come about when, through struggle and organizing, through memory and imagination, once-suppressed stories and voices are heard, their truth and validity recognized.

What Berry called the old story was a wall of noise shutting out yet older stories. Often, some of the genuinely new stories reinforce ancient cosmologies—notably the biological science offering a view of nature that accords well with many of the premodern stories describing a more symbiotic, interconnected, sentient world that was and is often a more egalitarian one. The increasing impact of contemporary Indigenous and non-Western, especially Buddhist, worldviews on the dominant culture is also significant. If the very new stories and the very old stories have so much in common, then the overarching story might be that somehow colonial industrial civilization was an epic mistake, or many kinds of mistake, a veering off course—and at least some of us are embarked on an epic course correction, or at least a heroic attempt to make one, through stories and ideas that are the seeds that become laws, practices, norms, and other parts of everyday life, and have succeeded, to a greater extent than is often realized.

These stories older than Berry's old story, the many stories subjugated under the one story, have influenced the new story. "One no and many yeses" and "a world where many worlds fit," said the Zapatistas, whose 1994 revolution in southern Mexico was a revolution of ideas and metaphors and frameworks heard around the world, as well as an uprising by Indigenous people that succeeded in establishing autonomous self-governed communities still standing (if embattled) more than thirty years later. Both these phrases of theirs could describe the decay of the one story and the rise of the many stories.

What was the land return at San Antonio Estero that windy day but the fruit of a new story? Or a story new to the dominant culture, since it was also about admitting back into audibility and agency people who had not forgotten the old stories about the land and their relationship to it? Much of what is new in mainstream society, in the dominant culture, is the return of the old ways, the ideas, stories, dreams, values that were not forgotten but pushed to the margins. Recognizing that means recognizing that colonial-industrial capitalism was an anomaly, an exceptionally destructive way of organizing consciousness and culture. We have new stories, and we have stories older than Berry's old story. We have stories. They are seeds with which to plant forests of possibility.

3

Varieties of Invisibility

There are many forms of invisibility, intentional and accidental. Some things are unrecognizable because they are outside the viewer's previous experience or frame of reference. When I visited Japan on the first anniversary of the triple catastrophe on March 11, 2011, of the Tōhoku earthquake, a tsunami, and a radioactive accident at the Fukushima nuclear power plant, a city administrator told me that when he saw a black wall of water more than seventy feet high coming at him and his coastal town of Otsuchi, it was so unbelievable he didn't recognize what it was at first. He did in time, took shelter, and survived, though 1,500 residents of Otsuchi, 10 percent of the town's population, did not. When I visited, the shards and ruins of what had been whole neighborhoods of Otsuchi still spread across the valley. Some didn't see the tsunami, or didn't have time to escape, or didn't escape to a safe enough place. Along Japan's eastern coast, some assumed it would go no further or higher than those in recent memory and sought refuge at what had in recent times been a safe enough location, or they trusted sea walls to protect them. But the recent past was not a good guide to the future that came rushing in.

Just before the 2016 election, I kept running into people with confidence that Hillary Clinton's predicted 85 percent chance of winning the election was as good as 100 percent. Like some of the people facing that black wall of water, they believed that the future could not be a shocking departure from the past, that the likely was the same as the inevitable, that the improbable was the same as the impossible. But history is full of things that once seemed unlikely; only our adjustment to them makes us forget how unforeseen or transgressive or transformative they were when they first appeared. In the age of climate change, we are embarking on a future that even physically, even where coastlines are and species thrive and how seasons unfold, will not look like the past.

About a decade ago, I spent some time scouring English-language news media from the spring and summer before the extraordinary autumn of 1989. That was when the authoritarian regimes of Poland, East Germany, Czechoslovakia, Hungary, Bulgaria, and Romania collapsed, thanks to their citizens' largely nonviolent direct action rooted in years and sometimes decades of quiet organizing. So far as I could tell, no one saw it coming, not even the participants, not with the sudden force it had, a political tsunami that swept away decades of Soviet domination not long before the Soviet Union itself dissolved. Perhaps underlying that obliviousness is the assumption that we might be at the end of something—even the end of time, for those fond of apocalypse and doom—but couldn't possibly be at the beginning of something else. We assume that the present is not in labor to bring forth a future unlike itself—and it is easier to see the old world dying than the new world being born. But beginnings are what come after endings.

One version of too big to see is a matter of size, of phenomena bigger than our senses can take in. Another kind of vastness is not spatial but temporal: change that can only be seen on the scale of decades or centuries, patterns and impacts that are only observable at scale. The status of women may seem stable on the scale of a year or a few years; on the scale of several decades, the change is staggering. In journalism, news is something that happens suddenly and recently, which works well for some kinds of violence, for elections or the passage of legislation (if not for the years-long journey that legislation often takes before it is passed and the campaigns and shifts in values even before that). But news doesn't work for ongoing incremental change, unless a milestone is selected and measured—a legislature has become 50 percent women, a temperature record has been broken. A change that seems sudden is often the result of years or decades or centuries of activity, often an accumulation of small and unnoticed shifts, like the tension that builds up until it produces an earthquake.

To cite a specific milestone, in the US in 2024, solar and wind outstripped coal as a source of electricity generation, and that September the United Kingdom—where the Industrial Revolution began, where everything ran on coal, where cities were blackened with the stuff for a century—closed its last coal-burning power plant. We are well into an energy revolution in which renewables are the inevitable future because they are simply the cheapest and best—as in cleanest, safest, most widely distributed, least environmentally destructive—way to make electricity, and it turns out that machines, including cars and stoves, that run on electricity are far more efficient than the fossil-fuel versions.

At the beginning of the millennium, there was no real climate solution; solar panels and wind turbines were expensive, ineffective technologies, and the emphasis was on austerity—if we had to use fossil fuel, maybe we could use less. Sadly, many people's understanding remains anchored in this era; the abundance that the absolutely free, almost universally distributed, and inexhaustible sun and wind can bring is still not adequately recognized. (Of course while the sunlight and wind are themselves free, it costs money to build the systems to turn them into electricity and distribute it. But once the systems are up and running, if they are not run by for-profit entities, they can be astonishingly inexpensive.) Somehow, an energy revolution took place through the efforts of engineers and inventors and the support of legislators, funders, and campaigners, and virtually every estimate of the drop in prices and rise in implementation of solar energy has been an immense underestimate. The advances have consistently outstripped the predictions; the future has proven more radical than the imagination of those contemplating and calculating it.

As Bill McKibben wrote in the summer of 2025, "In the past two years, however, with surprisingly little notice, renewable energy has suddenly become the obvious, mainstream, cost-efficient choice around the world." He added, "It took from the invention of the photovoltaic solar cell, in 1954, until 2022 for the world to install a terawatt of solar power; the second terawatt came just two years later, and the third will arrive either later this year or early next. That's because people are now putting up a gigawatt's worth of solar panels, the rough equivalent of the power generated by one coal-fired plant, every fifteen hours. Solar power is now growing faster than any power source in history, and it is closely followed by wind power. Last year, 96 percent of the global demand for new electricity was met by renewables." The rapid rise of large-scale battery storage, when coupled with solar, means that the sun can now shine at night—and it does in California, where batteries are often the main source of nocturnal electricity.

It's only the political power of the fossil fuel industry that is holding back a swifter transition to a renewable future. I regularly see articles describing the change over a year or two but almost nothing describing the breakthroughs and transitions that made possible the shift to a renewable future that has been underway over the past quarter century. So, a spectacular and encouraging transformation of the possibilities is largely invisible to the public because it's slow, technical, incremental, and because it's routinely described in short timespans rather than as a single long trajectory.

Change itself can be invisible without a baseline from which to measure. If, for example, you haven't lived somewhere for very long, you may assume its weather patterns and seasons are normal, while a longtime resident (or someone who listens to old-timers or studies the charts) may know that they are a departure from, and a disruption of, the norm. Amnesia can normalize the present while erasing the changes that led to it or the possibility of changing it again, which is why memory and history pose threats to authoritarian regimes. But other forces can lead to that amnesia.

In this historical moment, the way that a significant subset of men in the English-speaking world and beyond have turned to a particularly virulent and furious form of misogyny, spread on the internet, often by opportunists seeking to profit from and weaponize loneliness and confusion, is important news. But it is the nature of news itself to focus on what has gone wrong, and too often to also suggest it's new. The tactics and technologies are new, but this is only a regression to old forms of misogyny in which women were routinely described as separate and inferior species to be subjugated and exploited. Perhaps when something is no longer established and accepted, it has to fight hard for its agenda, when once that agenda was guaranteed: this is the lash in backlash.

While the focus on this new eruption is absolutely warranted, it obscures the fact that the majority of men have, over the past half century or so, actually accepted and internalized a lot of feminist ideas. It's why they treat women and girls differently than they did in the past, when many forms of inequality, exclusion, objectification, and denigration were normalized and unquestioned until feminism raised the questions. A lot of men have changed their own roles in domestic life, notably around parenting—men in heterosexual households still do less parenting and housework than women, overall, but the standards around what they should do and what role they should play in their children's lives have shifted significantly.

Perhaps these ideas are no longer feminist, in the sense of belonging to a movement or particular ideology, because they've been incorporated into the mainstream. In 1972, on arch-liberal Norman Lear's hugely influential TV show *All in the Family*, the daughter poses a riddle to her husband, mother, and father—or what at the time was perceived as a riddle: a father and son are in a car accident in which the father dies and the son is rushed to a hospital. In the hospital, the surgeon called in says, "I can't operate on this boy; he's my son." That the surgeon might be the boy's mother was an answer out of reach for a lot of people, including the *All in the Family* characters to whom the riddle was posed. In 2023, an older man on another liberal TV show, *Ted Lasso*, tries to pose the same anecdote as a riddle, but this time the joke is that the answer is immediately obvious to his listeners because female surgeons are now common.

So many things feed forgetting and undermine memory, including news that reports the events of the moment without the context that gives them coherence by showing the patterns into which they fit. Often, journalists pursue this stripping away of context in the name of objectivity or merely out of norms of what news is. The very term *news* evokes the new, while the understanding of what just happened requires knowing sources, context, evolutions of an idea or a piece of legislation or a career or campaign. Generational segregation deprives younger people of hearing from their elders about change, or so I would like to believe, but a lot of older people seem to perceive the rollercoaster of history we're all on as if we were standing still on solid ground.

I often have the sense that a lot of the people I read and listen to and talk with don't see the patterns, don't have a perspective that grasps the scale of change. For them, the present seems to be perpetual, unchanging, unyielding, offering confidence or despair that the future will be like the present, a conclusion that seems to be drawn from the lack of recognition that the present is a radical departure from the past. In this viewless view, no old world is dying, no new world is being born, though this short-term perspective doesn't exclude the monsters; it just makes them inexplicable and maybe undefeatable.

If knowledge is power, memory and perspective are among its most important aspects. Only in the long view can you see the patterns emerging, the way the present builds on the past, the way past surprises guarantee more surprises are coming, the ingredients of change over years, decades, centuries. If you don't see time on the scale of change, you don't see change; if you don't remember how things used to be, you don't know they're different than they were and how that unfolded. While some people are too young to remember the past firsthand (and some know it other ways), I'm often struck by my peers who've lived through dizzying change and somehow adjusted without noticing it.

I remember how the economic policies of Ronald Reagan created mass homelessness, but if you forget that, you can imagine homelessness is inevitable or the result of personal failings or local conditions, not primarily a creation of the radical rearrangement of the national economy in pursuit of a return to the old inequality (and similar cuts to social services in other countries produced similar forms of desperation and displacement). From the 1930s through the 1970s, from the New Deal to the War on Poverty, the US government created more social safety nets and more economic equality, lifting up the poor and taxing the rich. Beginning in the 1980s, these achievements were dismantled, and new policies created a more unequal, insecure society. To remember that this was created by specific decisions is to remember that it can be changed again; to remember that something once existed—like California's tuition-free public universities—is to remember that it can exist again.

Another form change takes is cessation. To see the absence of something, you must remember that it was once present and maybe how it was eradicated. As has often been said, the now all too common dismissal of or outright opposition to vaccines seems drawn in part from forgetting the devastation wrought by many diseases such as measles, polio, and smallpox before vaccines for them were developed and vaccine campaigns had their impact. Sometimes the sense that a movement has failed or not mattered comes from forgetting its victories and what those victories were against. To notice that something does not happen anymore, be it a disease, an assumption, a kind of persecution, or anything else, you have to remember it used to happen. It's also easy to overlook that what is with us now is here because of past efforts, the kinds that prevented the trees from being cut down, a species from going extinct, services from being cut, institutions from being shut down.

A pattern can only be seen at scale; if you only see a fragment, you miss the pattern. I wrote a few years ago that I often feel like a tortoise at a mayfly party, a slow creature lumbering through the long term among people flitting around in the immediate. But it feels weirder than that now, like one of those movies where one person sees what those around her don't. It might be a ghost movie, but it's not a horror movie: much of what I see is good. More than good—miraculous, awe-inspiring. I see the roots of twenty-first century movements in the twentieth and even the nineteenth and sometimes the eighteenth, see the idea of human rights lurch forward from time to time over the centuries, assume that process is far from over in the present. How something said to have failed before it's really begun can go dormant for years or decades and then resume. How one transformation can open up the possibility of further transformations, just as one shift in perception makes it possible to see what was hitherto invisible and thereby generates further shifts. How change begets itself, feeds on itself, rides itself—guided, manipulated, orchestrated, but in some ways driven by an internal momentum.

I see how indirect consequences mean that something can have an impact that's not linear—for example, you may not win the battle, but you may inspire others to join the war or fight and win other battles. I've seen other campaigns fail to realize a specific victory but be part of the larger transformation of values and visions. I've also been fortunate enough to see environmental campaigns that have lasted three decades or more achieve their victory at last.

I have seen history itself unfold, and this witness has been one of the things that brings purpose and exhilaration to my life as a writer and a citizen of this earth. I have seen change. As Jonathan Schell once wrote of how revolutions unfold in the imagination first, "Individual hearts and minds change; those who have changed become aware of one another; still others are emboldened, in a contagion of boldness; the 'impossible' becomes possible; immediately it is done, surprising the actors almost as much as their opponents, and suddenly, almost with the swiftness of thought—whose transformation has in fact set the whole process in motion—the old regime, a moment ago so impressive, vanishes like a mirage." Not always. But sometimes.

I've traced with pleasure how British suffragists protesting for the right to vote in London influenced a young Indian lawyer who had just arrived in that country after organizing his first protest against injustice in South Africa. He was, of course, Mohandas Gandhi, whose theory and practice of nonviolence was hugely influential on, among other things, the Black civil rights movement in the US, which, in turn, influenced other human rights movements in the US and around the world into the present—so, the answer to the question, "What did those women in London achieve?" is, arguably, still being answered, ideas and tools of liberation being passed from movement to movement.

Which reminds me, in turn, of how Zhou Enlai, the inaugural premier of the People's Republic of China, was once asked what he thought of the French Revolution, and he replied, "Too soon to tell." In some versions of this story he is referring to the 1789 revolution, but more reliable sources seem to suggest he was addressing the 1968 uprisings. That long view is the antithesis of the summary judgments I often encounter on things that are far from done or even hardly begun, the premature surrender, the expectation that if results aren't instant and obvious there are none.

I see the immense impact of human rights campaigns, including antiracist, feminist, immigrant, disability-rights, and queer-rights movements; see the rise of environmental awareness and its application in creating laws and systems to protect the natural world and their consequence as protected places and species and systems; see decolonization as an actual shift in governance over huge territories in my lifetime but also a decolonization of the imagination; see the slow decline or maybe denormalization of authoritarianism, in the home and in personal relationships as well as in public life. (And denormalization is a crucial tool for change, for making what had long been unquestioned or acceptable or even invisible less so while also dreaming and imagining—and proposing—that things could be otherwise.) Not all the changes have been for the better, of course, but those that have been share underlying values of equality, inclusion, empathy, the delegitimization of violence, and beneath those values a belief in interconnection.

The existence of these wonderful things does not erase or render insignificant the terrible ones, nor are any of them realized in complete and perfect ways, or unchallenged. To say that things have changed is not to say that the change is finished or is complete, or that all things have changed for the better, when so many things have so obviously changed for the worse (a caveat I have been declaring one way or another for decades, because I've encountered, often enough and then some, the habit of turning my "some things are good" and "some things got better" into "she said everything is good and everything is better but it's not"). Out of this sea of change I want to trace some threads and try to describe the tapestry they weave, the patterns they make.

4

A Single Garment
of Destiny

Sometimes there is a poetic beauty to the truth that everything is connected. When the problem is contamination, the news of inseparability is instead a nightmare. I don't know what a third of a million baby teeth—deciduous teeth, the scientists called them—would look like or how much room they would take up. I know that in the late 1950s, scientists in St. Louis, Missouri, collected almost that many—320,000—from local children, parents, and dentists to measure them for radiation contamination.

More than a thousand nuclear bombs were detonated in the southern Nevada desert from 1951 to 1991. These were full-scale atomic bomb explosions, most of them far larger than the bombs that destroyed Hiroshima and Nagasaki. Before 1963, a hundred above-ground nuclear bombs were set off there, so bright they could be seen from hundreds of miles away (or, for many soldiers forced to witness them up close, so bright the soldiers saw the bones of their hands through their closed eyes). They also begat clouds of radioactive particles that rained down across the continent—mostly carried east by the prevailing winds during the tests.

Strontium-90 was one of the products of nuclear fission that fell from these clouds, and, as cows grazed contaminated grass, the radioactive strontium concentrated—bioaccumulated, as scientists put it—and showed up in cow's milk and human milk. Bodies mistook the element for calcium and incorporated it into bones. Lost baby teeth were an accessible way to study its accumulation in human bones, so the collecting began in 1958. The study was perhaps the first of that era to convey that ignoring interconnection came at a cost.

Rachel Carson mentions strontium-90 on page 6 of her book *Silent Spring*, published in September 1962. The book is well remembered for waking up the public to the dangers of the herbicides and pesticides used so profligately in the 1950s, especially the then widely used and extremely effective insecticide DDT. She wrote that the chemicals deployed actually did their intended job extremely well, at least at first: they killed unwanted plants and insects (though the insects sometimes later developed resistance). The problem was that the chemicals didn't stop there.

They kept killing: they killed natural predators of the targeted insects, including birds and other insects, went into the plants, the soil, the water, killed whole riversful of fish, killed more birds, sometimes killed humans exposed to heavy doses. "A sample of drinking water from an orchard area in Pennsylvania, when tested on fish in a laboratory, contained enough insecticide to kill all of the test fish in only four hours," Carson wrote. "Water from a stream draining sprayed cotton fields remained lethal to fishes even after it had passed through a purifying plant, and in fifteen streams tributary to the Tennessee River in Alabama the runoff from fields treated with toxaphene, a chlorinated hydrocarbon, killed all the fish inhabiting the streams. Two of these streams were sources of municipal water supply."

She told a story of how the Forest Service sprayed ten thousand acres with an herbicide that was supposed to kill sagebrush, to turn land in Wyoming's Bridger National Forest into better grasslands for cattle. The sagebrush died. The poison also killed willows that grew alongside the streams. When the willows died, the moose and beaver vanished, and when the beaver vanished, so did their dams that had created pools and ponds, and with those gone, the trout disappeared. "None could live in the tiny creek that remained, threading its way through a bare, hot land where no shade remained," she wrote.

The book's title came from an opening scene imagining a spring without birdsong, though birds higher up the food chain than songbirds were most impacted—hawks, eagles, pelicans—because, at each link of that chain, the chemicals concentrated. DDT made those wild birds' eggshells so thin and fragile they often broke in the nest before hatching. Peregrine falcons became extinct in the eastern US and southeastern Canada, bald eagle and brown pelican populations crashed.

Carson's earlier books had been lushly poetic descriptions of the sea and seashore that won her a huge readership, but *Silent Spring* was a sober book in which she mounted a case like a lawyer, with example after example of devastation through industrial chemicals and explanations of their workings. The book had a substantial index and fifty-four pages of bibliography, mostly scientific studies. She knew she'd come under attack from the chemical industry and its supporters, and she may have known she'd also come under attack for her gender (as she was, in review after review that patronized her, called her hysterical, treated her as unqualified, ignored that she was a scientist with a master's degree in biology from Johns Hopkins University—only poverty had prevented her from completing a PhD—who had worked as an aquatic biologist for the US Fish and Wildlife Service for almost two decades).

The one story she told over and over again was that everything is connected, that the poisons intended to kill unwanted insects or plants keep traveling through air, soil, water, and the bodies of plants and animals, including humans: "The fact that every meal we eat carries its load of chlorinated hydrocarbons is the inevitable consequence of the almost universal spraying or dusting of agricultural crops with these poisons." Elsewhere, she declared, "Can anyone believe it is possible to lay down such a barrage of poisons on the surface of the earth without making it unfit for all life? They should not be called 'insecticides,' but 'biocides.'" Killers of life.

That everything is connected to everything else is fundamental to environmental science, and in a healthy ecosystem there's a poetry to how the many parts of the system interact to mutual benefit. My eleven-year-old great-niece recently told me what had been taught to her in elementary school: reintroducing wolves to Yellowstone National Park (in 1995) curbed the elk population and kept it moving, which let the willow, aspen, and cottonwood saplings grow by the streams, which provided beaver with the material for dams, which created ponds and wetlands, which increased the habitat for fish and songbirds, and benefited the system as a whole. That had been big news and, for some, a big and controversial concept a few decades ago; that it was now taught in fifth grade was a sign of how an idea migrates and settles in.

Carson wrote in an era in which environmental knowledge was far from widespread—and by environmental knowledge I mean recognizing nature as a system, recognizing interconnection, consequences, relationships, that all parts of a system have a role in that system, and tinkering with any part of that system impacts the whole. There was, before Carson, no environmental movement and little environmental awareness, and words like *food chain*, *bioaccumulate*, *downstream* were not in the public's vocabulary, though atomic testing had taught them *downwind*.

In that era, the conservation movement was concerned with setting aside exceptionally splendid or unique places to be preserved while, all too often, smiling upon the development and industrialization of the rest. (It has since grown more sophisticated about why and how to protect places and which ones merit protection.) Industrialists, financiers, and businessmen involved in extractive industries were often the patrons or board members of these organizations, which, by setting aside some places tacitly and sometimes directly, consented to and participated in exploitation of the rest. It was a politics of sequestration, of separation.

The environmental movement would be its opposite, increasingly recognizing over the decades after *Silent Spring* that you could not separate anything from anything else, ecologically, and that to protect even the remotest places or their species, you have to address the system as a whole, that what we mine or burn or spray or detonate here will end up there. In 1970, scientist and environmental visionary Barry Commoner wrote up "the four laws of ecology," of which the first is "Everything is connected to everything else."

Commoner was one of the scientists in St. Louis, Missouri, who, along with Dr. Louise Reiss and Ursula Franklin, launched the Greater St. Louis Citizens' Committee for Nuclear Information in 1958, while Carson was just beginning *Silent Spring*. The committee sought to study nuclear contamination from fallout in their region, and to that end collected those 320,000 baby teeth. Their analysis demonstrated that levels of strontium-90 in the teeth, and therefore in the children they came from, had risen dramatically during the 1950s. Their reports in 1961 and 1963 had a huge impact. Activists, including Women Strike for Peace, a nationwide feminist antinuclear and antiwar group founded in 1961, used that data in their campaigns. One result of the public outcry was that, in 1963, the Partial Nuclear Test Ban Treaty put US and Soviet nuclear tests underground, significantly reducing the radioactive fallout from the bombs.

Martin Luther King Jr. remarked in that period, "One cannot be concerned just with civil rights. It is very nice to drink milk at an unsegregated lunch counter—but not when there's strontium-90 in it." The sit-ins at segregated lunch counters across the South had begun in early 1960, as the civil rights movement gained momentum. Six months after *Silent Spring* appeared, King wrote in his "Letter from a Birmingham Jail" that "we are caught in an inescapable network of mutuality, tied in a single garment of destiny. Whatever affects one directly, affects all indirectly." It is the best-known but not the first time he used the "single garment of destiny" sentence, which so well expressed his theology that he used it over and over again in the sermons and speeches he gave across the country in the five years before his murder in 1968.

While King is remembered as a visionary champion of civil rights, the heart of his vision was not just of rights but of interconnectedness (and he and Carson converged even in their metaphors: she wrote of the "whole closely knit fabric of life" being "ripped apart"). When he used those two sentences in the 1961 sermon "The Man Who Was a Fool," he followed them with "I can never be what I ought until you are what you ought to be, and you can never be what you ought until I am what I ought to be. This is the interrelated structure of reality." He urged a universal love, a love without borders, a love that did not stop because of another race or nationality or religion.

He sought both to take down the legal, political, and conceptual barriers and to encourage and celebrate the love that was not stopped by them. His introduction of nonviolence as both ethic and strategy drew from Mohandas Gandhi's *satyagraha*, often translated as soul force, though King called it truth force and love force. In his book about the 1955 Montgomery Bus Boycott, King wrote that "Gandhi was probably the first person in history to lift the love ethic of Jesus above mere interaction between individuals to a powerful and effective social force on a large scale."

He saw his age as a transformative one, preaching (in words that echo Gramsci's) in 1956, "Those of us who lived in the twentieth century are privileged to live in one of the most momentous periods of human history. It is an exciting age, filled with hope. It is an age in which a new world order is being born. We stand today between two worlds—the dying old and the emerging new. I am aware of the fact that there are those who would argue that we live in the most ghastly period of human history. . . . They would argue that we are going backwards instead of forward, that we are retrogressing instead of progressing. But far from representing retrogression or tragic hopelessness, the present tension represents the necessary pains that accompany the birth of anything new. . . . We are all familiar with this old world that is dying, the old world that is passing away, we have lived with it, we have seen it, we look out and see it in its international proportion and we see it in the form of colonialism and imperialism."

"We live in one world geographically. We face the great problem of making it one spiritually," he declared in 1956, speaking of protests and boycotts as part of the birth pains, of liberation from oppression, and asserting that "the end is reconciliation. The end is the creation of a beloved community."

Decades later, the Detroit-based political philosopher Grace Lee Boggs saw the Montgomery Bus Boycott King helped launch as the beginning of a new way of thinking and organizing. Boggs, who lived from 1915 to 2015 and evolved from an orthodox Marxist into a visionary community organizer, wrote late in her long life that the bus boycott was "the first struggle by an oppressed people in Western society from this new philosophical/political perspective.

Before the eyes of the whole world, a people who had been treated as less than human struggled against their dehumanization not as angry victims or rebels but as new men and women, representative of a new, more human society." They acted, in other words, not only on the basis of the rights they lacked, but on the spiritual strength they had in abundance; acted to take and also to give.

Nonviolence was a strategy for the less powerful to resist the more powerful while also refusing to see them as the enemy. Boggs continues, "Their goal was not only desegregating the buses but creating the beloved community." Later, we'd come to call that pre-figurative politics, the way that you can and should embody what you aspire to. King did much to make the Montgomery boycott the visionary struggle it was, and it did much to make him the catalyst for change he became. The beloved community was his idea of both what the goal should be for society as a whole and what the move-ment could embody in its practices and values. It was a vision of love beyond the personal and private realms where it is most often recognized and validated, a community-based love, a public love, an inclusive love, ultimately a divine love without limits. He saw it in action in Montgomery, writing, "Men and women who had been separated from each other by false standards of class were now singing and praying together in a common struggle for freedom and human dignity."

Theologians contemplating the beloved community note that King aspired to change more than laws: "Whereas desegregation can be brought about by laws, integration requires a change in atti-tudes. It involves personal and social relationships that are created by love—and these cannot be legislated. Integration will enlarge 'the concept of brotherhood to a vision of total interrelatedness.'" While some Black rights activists were separatists, King was always an integrationist; his goal was to dismantle social and racial divides and the imaginative and ethical ones reinforcing them. And he recognized, as many campaigners in the 1960s did not, that change had to happen on deeper levels than that of laws.

The Montgomery Bus Boycott did not come out of nowhere. Behind every beginning is another beginning, another story. For decades, the stories most widely told about Rosa Parks reduced her to a tired seamstress acting on impulse or out of personal grievance when she refused to yield her seat to a white person at the bus driver's command and was arrested on December 1, 1955. That story erased that her act was part of a system and movement. She was, in fact, a courageous and important organizer with the NAACP, who had since the 1940s focused on something the new phase of the civil rights movement didn't mention much: the rape of Black women by white men across the South as part of a racial order in which the former were as lacking in rights and power as the latter were free from accountability.

A hero is herself part of a system, or rather the system makes her a hero, a catalyst for something bigger than herself. If a stone is thrown into a lake, it's the water that's splashing, then rippling outward, not the stone. When Greta Thunberg, at fifteen, sat down with a cardboard sign to protest inaction on climate change, it was the way that the media and the public responded to her, the way she captured public imagination, the way young people across the world launched their own Friday for Future protests, that made her protest matter. She was far from the first youth climate protestor, but she may have come along when the world was finally ready to listen.

When Rosa Parks sat down after work on a Thursday, she stood up, and many members of the Black community stood with her. The Women's Political Council of Montgomery immediately mimeographed and distributed leaflets to the Black community to organize a bus boycott, and other community members organized transportation for those who joined the boycott the following Monday. The bus boycott transformed King into a national and then an international figure (who received the Nobel Peace Prize in 1964), and the nonviolence he learned in part from reading Gandhi and Henry David Thoreau begat organizing strategies used around the world ever since.

But had hundreds, then tens of thousands, then millions not joined him, King would be an eloquent voice, not a catalyst. In much the same way, the impact of *Silent Spring* lay in the public response to it, which led to Carson's congressional testimony (and it's worth remembering that both of them faced tremendous pushback and, in King's case, years of threats of violence and a stabbing before the bullet that ended his life in 1968). In his book *The Unconquerable World*, Jonathan Schell declared that nonviolence and nuclear weapons were the two most significant creations of the twentieth century, the former having more power and the latter less than was commonly assumed.

In King's 1961 sermon "On Being a Good Neighbor," he noted that Athenian democracy was only for an elite, and though American democracy was launched with the declaration that "all men are created equal," it excluded Black men—to which, in our era, he might have added Native Americans and women of all races. He noted, "The good neighbor looks beyond the external accidents and discerns those inner qualities that make all men human and, therefore, brothers." Elsewhere, he declared, "Through our scientific and technological genius, we have made of this world a neighborhood and yet we have not had the ethical commitment to make of it a brotherhood."* He was struck, again and again, by how the world

---

* King, like James Baldwin and others of their era, routinely used phrases like *mankind, man, brotherhood,* to mean all of humanity, and *the Black man* to

had changed to make us all more interconnected, and how this was a practical, political, and economic reality but insufficiently a moral and social reality.

While he used metaphors drawn from nature and found pleasure and solace in the natural world, his focus was on the human. But there's still a case to be made that, like Carson, he was an environmental thinker in his recognition of interconnection or what his friend the Vietnamese Buddhist teacher Thich Nhat Hanh called "interbeing." King signed on with the antinuclear movements of the 1950s and recognized the harm in fallout. Had he lived longer, many of us believe he would have supported environmental and then climate action; while he lived, he broadened his vision from civil rights to economic justice to antiwar activism.

King scholar Drew Dellinger writes, "As early as the Montgomery Bus Boycott in 1956, King said, 'The fact that this new age is emerging reveals something basic about the universe. It tells us something about the core and heartbeat of the cosmos.' . . . Along with his well-known worldview of prophetic Christianity, interconnection and interdependence were central to his thinking, and consistent themes in his rhetoric. King saw reality as an interlacing network of relationships, viewed the nations and peoples of the planet as one, and linked various social injustices, saying, 'All of these problems are tied together.'"

He was antiracist, antiwar, and anticolonial, influenced by India's liberation from British colonialism, closely following decolonization struggles in Africa and Asia, traveling to Ghana in 1957 to celebrate its independence. Though he didn't talk about protecting the environment, his vision was deeply ecological in the sense

---

mean all Black people, before feminism noted that this language promulgated the idea that men were the norm or archetype or subject while sidelining or erasing women.

of Commoner's "everything is connected to everything else" and his work against segregation and division. Sometimes we call that systemic thinking or an ecological vision, as it was for Carson. King called that principle of connection and care *love*.

5

Shadows of the Past

In so many ways, the world in which King and Carson lived and died was not the world in which you're reading this. Almost everything has changed—unevenly, imperfectly, incompletely—but even so, the ways we think and talk about gender, race, sexuality, nature, agriculture and food, indigeneity, equality, family, violence, justice, and so much more have shifted in so many ways in the last several decades, as has who is included in many versions of "we." *Silent Spring* and "Letter from a Birmingham Jail" came out when I was a baby. I've lived through a lot of the changes they helped launch, most of them happening so incrementally that they unfolded invisibly, but a thousand steps add up to a considerable distance.

There were landmarks as legislation—the Civil Rights Act of 1964, the 1970 Clean Air Act and Clean Water Act, the DDT ban in the US in 1972—but that legislation didn't change people's minds. The changes in people's minds led to the legislation via the stories that got told, the values that got expressed, the relationships that got built, the way once-radical ideas became accepted norms and actualities (and often scholarship, research, writing, organizing, and campaigning changed the minds), the way that accepted norms and actualities got questioned, delegitimized, and then transformed. Sometimes the measure of these changes comes back

42

to me when I go back to works of art I loved. That I see them differently, see things I didn't see before, is a measure of not only how much I've changed but how much the society around me has changed, because my transformation wasn't individual. Like all of us, I was carried by the current.

One of my favorite childhood books was T. H. White's wittily reimagined Arthurian romance, *The Once and Future King*, but when, as an adult, I went back to it for what I remembered as a wise passage about the steadfastness that comes with middle age, I found a tiny jab in this sentence: "She no longer hopes to live by seeking the truth—if women ever do hope this—but continues henceforth under the guidance of a seventh sense." I wondered about how at maybe age eleven I'd taken this aside condemning the moral and intellectual capacity of my gender in stride, or rather how it impacted me, or didn't because I was so accustomed to being dismissed and excluded in these minor ways as well as some major ones.

I saw the film *Purple Rain*, starring Prince, in a movie theater when it came out in 1984. I still love Prince, and I loved the movie then, or so I recall. But when I decided a few years ago to watch it at home, thinking I'd still enjoy it, I got to the scene in which Prince's character convinces the female lead—a fellow musician who wants his help with her career while he apparently wants her, as in lusts after her—that there's an initiation ritual she needs to go through, whereby you jump naked into Lake Minnetonka. They arrive at the edge of a pond on the back of his motorcycle, where he urges her to strip down and jump in. When she does, he laughs at her, tells her it's not Lake Minnetonka, and rides away, leaving her wet, cold, stranded, and furious. Then he comes back. She says, "I must've looked pretty ridiculous," accepting the abuse, offering a smile as if she's the one who needs to smooth things over, and trying to get on the bike as he lurches forward a few times to stymie her again before they ride off.

I wondered who I'd been when I'd watched that film (and so many like it) all those years ago, mused over how I had not felt pangs at her treatment or even retained much of an impression of it. How had I somehow gone along with that film and so many others and all the novels and songs and the rest that convinced me to see things from the man's point of view or to find abuse acceptable? How had I seen women through men's eyes, over and over, as enigmatic cyphers and objects for consumption, not as part of the conversation, or missed that they (and by implication I) were thereby shut out?

Back then, if I'd protested, I would've been told that I was uptight, had no sense of humor, should be able to take a joke. But that's not it, either, because I don't think I'd really felt it; to feel all the insults and threats aimed at girls and women would have been more than I could have coped with, maybe more than I was equipped to cope with. The equipment would come later, and the space in which to use it. I'd never known anything else, and we would slowly, incrementally, break out of it together, step by step, first of all by describing what exactly was going on and why exactly we found it troubling—or were finally in a time and place where we could articulate that it was troubling and refuse to continue to smooth over and accept it. Denormalizing is important work.

In other respects, *Purple Rain* is, or at least aspires to be, a feminist movie, with women musicians who insist on their creative independence and a domestic violence subplot. And, of course, its stars are Black, and that was a breakthrough in an era when most movies had no Black characters and almost no films were centered on Black lives. It's a step along the road, even if it stumbles, and I don't mean to condemn the film or suggest that I was somehow injured or overwhelmed by it either time I watched it. I just find these returns to old works of art moments when I realize that I and the world have changed. I'm not alone. Molly Ringwald, who, as a teenager, starred in three hit films about teens in the mid-1980s—*Sixteen Candles, Pretty in Pink,* and *The Breakfast Club*—wrote an essay in 2018 about the exploitations and denigrations in them she found disturbing as an adult. They were things that she and we didn't much notice at the time, because they were normal and ubiquitous, because the critical insight and even the language to address what was cruel or unfair or exploitative in them wasn't yet available to most of us.

Change itself can be invisible without a baseline from which to measure, and maybe a baseline of that old world that some of us have departed from is worth establishing. I remember it from my own experience and from how it was described in books, films, songs of the era, in the norms and expectations of my youth. Looking back, it seems most of all a world of division and compartmentalization, of tidy categories to keep us apart, keep us in our place and keep many of us out of many places, framed as natural and inevitable and necessary to maintaining order. Change would be framed as disorder by those who sought to stop it. Some of it was as public as the Jim Crow laws Rosa Parks and Martin Luther King Jr. organized to overturn; some of it was as subtle as the social norms in everyday life and art.

A year before *Silent Spring* and two before "Letter from a Birmingham Jail," the Berlin Wall went up, a fissure across a great city that came to represent the divide of Europe into the communist East and the capitalist West. The world itself was imagined as a sort of binary, neatly divided between capitalism and communism, and the United States intervened violently in Asia and Latin America in the name of preventing the expansion of the latter. Capitalist countries claimed that capitalism was inseparable from democracy, bolstered by the fact that most of the countries that were officially communist were functionally totalitarian.

The world was divided along racial lines in many ways and places. The United States was a far whiter, far more Christian country than it is now, and that white Protestants should dominate and impose their norms was implicit and explicit in many arenas and hierarchies. When John F. Kennedy ran for the presidency in 1960, his allegiance to the nation was questioned because he was Catholic, even though he'd served in the House, the Senate, and the US Navy (even Martin Luther King Jr.'s father hesitated to vote for a Catholic). Not long after Kennedy's election, the Protestant father of a friend of mine left his job as a corporate attorney in New York City for a position in San Francisco, because her nominally Catholic mother would never have been fully accepted in the swank circles they moved in in the former city. The difference between ethnic whites—Catholic, Jewish, Irish, Eastern or Southern European—and elite Protestants mattered then.

Into the late 1960s and 1970s, Ivy League and other elite private universities only admitted men as undergraduates, largely white men, and some of them had quotas to limit the number of Jews. Legacy admissions—admitting students because their fathers (later, parents) had gone there—was and is one way of maintaining the homogeneity and practicing affirmative action for white mediocrity. Across the nation, private clubs, resorts, hotels, and neighborhood housing covenants also kept out Jews, and many forms of official segregation as well as unofficial intimidation and menace kept Black and brown people out of white neighborhoods, organizations, and public spaces, including pools and beaches. Redlining—preventing access to loans, insurance, and other financial services, or offering overpriced and inferior versions—helped keep Black neighborhoods poor, and helped keep Black people in those neighborhoods, which often had less (or no) access to good schools, good grocery stores, parks, and public services.

Jim Crow cut far more harshly across southern society, segregating hospitals, schools, drinking fountains, and theaters, preventing Blacks from voting through poll taxes and rigged literacy tests and through threat and violence and unequal protection under the law, keeping Black people out of professions, jobs, and businesses. In 1967, the *Loving v. Virginia* case in the Supreme Court overturned state bans on interracial marriage in seventeen states. (Mildred Jeter Loving, who was Indigenous and Black, and Richard Loving, who was white, had been arrested in 1958 and threatened with a year in prison, to be suspended if they left the state for twenty-five years under a Virginia law on the books since 1662. After years of exile from their rural people and place, the ACLU took their case and won it, and they were able to return home.) Questioned in the public discourse, challenged by the movements, fought in the courts, the categories were breaking open.

Endless pictures of boards of directors, senates, cabinets, judge benches, and other powerful groups featured, from the founding of the country into the present, oceans of white male faces.* That this could and should change was only beginning to be discussed in the 1960s. The inequality and exclusion of women from avenues of power was so normalized by law and custom that feminists would spend decades even trying to recognize, name, and denormalize the exclusions and change the laws. Almost no women served in the higher ranks of government and industry. Discrimination in hiring

---

* The first Black man on the Supreme Court came in 1967; the first woman in 1981, and the first Black woman in 2022. The first Black man to hold a cabinet position in a US administration was in 1966; the first Black woman in 1977. The first Black CEO of a Fortune 500 company came in 1987; the first Black woman to hold such a position only in 2009.

and employment was legal and common, and newspapers some-times listed jobs for men and women separately (early second-wave feminists protested the *New York Times* for this policy in 1967). Women had no right to equal pay or equal advancement on their qualifications before the Equal Pay Act of 1963.

In the US until 1978, women could be fired for being pregnant. Gloria Steinem reported in 1969, "Forty-three states have 'protection legislation' limiting the hours and place a woman can work; legislation that is, as Governor Rockefeller admitted last year, 'more often protective of men.'" Sexual harassment in the workplace was the subject of smirking cartoons in magazines, usually some version of a portly middle-aged white man in a suit chasing a pretty young white woman around a desk. Before Anita Hill spoke up in 1991, testifying in the Senate hearings on Clarence Thomas's nomination to the Supreme Court that he had sexually harassed her when they worked together in the 1980s, little was done to acknowledge or prevent it. In the 1980 comedic movie *Nine to Five*, about three secretaries and an abusive lecherous boss, they take matters into their own hands—they kidnap him—in part because there were almost no other options on the table. I was sexually harassed in workplaces in those pre-1991 days, and my only available option was to strategize how to rebuff the lechers without infuriating them, since that could be dangerous to my employment or to me personally.

Women were supposed to be physically, intellectually, and emotionally feeble compared to men, the justification for keeping women out of sports, the military, the professions (including medicine and law), graduate education, management positions, and much more. (At the University of Virginia in the late nineteenth century, instruction of women was denied on the grounds that education "does often physically unsex them, and they afterwards fail in the demands of motherhood.") Women were routinely treated as less reliable, objective, competent, and rational than men, and belittlement was routine—Rachel Carson, for example, was often described in print as overwrought and incompetent to address the science of her subject, though she was an experienced scientist calmly assembling a factual case against pesticides and herbicides in *Silent Spring*.

On June 14, 1968, Mississippi became the last state in the union to overturn a law preventing women from serving on juries. A year before, Texas had passed a law giving married women independent financial agency; Louise Ballerstedt Raggio, the lawyer who wrote that legislation had, earlier in her career, needed her husband to sign her clients' bail bonds because, as a wife in that state, she was not allowed to take independent financial action. "It was idiots, convicts, minors, and married women who didn't have property rights," she wrote in her autobiography.

Marriage was a legal contract and social arrangement in which women were expected to surrender their legal, social, bodily, and financial agency. It was normal for husbands to make major decisions without wives' knowledge or consent. In 1981, the Supreme Court overturned the last "head and master" law, in which the state gave sole control of marital property to the husband. (The lawsuit in question involved a Louisiana couple, in which the husband sold a house the wife had bought with her own earnings to pay for his defense against charges of sexually abusing their daughter.)

Marital rape was only recognized as such and then made a crime thanks to feminist work in the 1970s and 1980s. Domestic violence—then called wife beating—was illegal in some circumstances, but police forces and the legal system took little interest in protecting women from it; it was instead often treated jokily, or the woman was told to be more pleasing, more submissive. Battered women's shelters, restraining orders, laws about stalking and harassment, the very language for some of these things were creations of the women's movement.

The 1964 Supreme Court case *Griswold v. Connecticut* overturned the ban on birth control in that state but only for married couples; unmarried women still had trouble accessing it, and abortion remained largely illegal until yet another Supreme Court decision, 1973's *Roe v. Wade*, overturned in 2022. Perhaps a mistake of 1960s rights movements was believing that changing the law was enough; subsequent decades would demonstrate that changing the culture is also necessary, because you're never really equal under the law when you're unequal in the society.

There's a similar timeline for British women. In 1918, after decades of campaigns for female suffrage, property-owning women over thirty in the UK gained the right to vote, and all women over twenty-one did so in 1928; professions began opening to women, so that the first woman magistrate came in 1919, the same year the first woman was seated in Parliament, and the first woman was called to the bar in 1922. But many other forms of equality took half a century more to arrive—an equal pay act came in 1970, followed by the 1975 Sex Discrimination Act, preventing (in theory) discrimination in employment, education, and training; married women got the right to co-own any savings, but until 1970 women were still refused mortgages without a male cosigner, and it took until 1994 to make marital rape a crime. In 1967 came limited abortion rights, generally requiring the consent of two doctors (who, in that era, were likely to be male), but an 1861 law criminalizing "unlawful" abortions was overturned only as of 2025. Decriminalizing and granting equal rights to queer people progressed slowly, in the UK as in the US.

Into the 1970s, heterosexuality and heteronormative appearance and conduct were also strictly enforced by law and culture, with gay men in particular imprisoned, kicked out of the military and the teaching professions, gay bars raided, and both men and women criminalized for not dressing in the clothes conventional for their gender. That is to say, being queer was regarded as both a crime and a mental illness or moral failing, and most queer people lived covert, hidden lives, safe only in carefully managed circumstances, in fear of these punishments. (Until 1974, the *Diagnostic and Statistical Manual of Mental Disorders* [DSM], a standard reference volume for the US mental health industry, named homosexuality as a subset of "personality disorders"; its inclusion in the DSM was overturned by a vote among members of the American Psychiatric Association: 5,854 voted for removing it, 3,810 for retaining it.)

Even in the twenty-first century, the right to marriage equality was bitterly opposed by conservatives, perhaps motivated by how same-sex love threatened (and threatens) the sense of inevitability and fixity of traditional heterosexual gender roles, including inequality between the sexes. The justification for this discrimination has often been a claim about what is natural and what is nature; homosexuality was "a crime against nature" or included on lists of "unnatural acts." (As for what nature is and therefore what's natural, contemporary science recognizes considerable homoerotic activity and same-sex pair-bonding, as well as many forms of gender, including hermaphroditism and changes from one gender to another, in the animal kingdom.)

This is a baldly stated list of facts and for many readers a familiar one, but two things are striking to me about that era that shed light on our own. One is how much this world of airtight categories did not just separate people but stacked them up in hierarchies, white over Black, colonizers over the colonized, settler colonialists over Indigenous, straight over queer, male over female, bosses over employees, teachers over students, doctors over patients, police over citizens.

For example, in medicine as practiced before the 1970s, it was routine for doctors to decide not only what a patient's treatment should be but what, if anything, the patient should know about their diagnosis, including the nature of their disorder and whether it was terminal. That it is now routine and even required to fully disclose test results and diagnoses and involve adult patients in healthcare decisions is the result of an insufficiently remembered revolution in healthcare in which feminism played a significant part. (That women advocated for more agency in childbirth and reproductive care, as well as for better understanding of their own bodies and functions—through the famous manual *Our Bodies, Ourselves*, first published in the early 1970s, among other means—is well-known; that the women's health movement helped secure more agency for all patients is less recognized.)

In another example of institutional authoritarianism, violence against students under the bland rubric "corporal punishment" was routine in many public schools. In the early 1970s, two Florida boys who'd been beaten by officials in their junior high school, one of them severely enough to require hospitalization, filed suit on the grounds that their constitutional rights had been violated. In 1977, in *Ingraham v. Wright*, the Supreme Court found against them, ruling "there can be no deprivation of substantive rights as long as disciplinary corporal punishment is within the limits of common-law privilege." In other words, since instructors had always beaten students, students could always be beaten.

The exercise of authority, the right of some to control others, the expectation that subordinates should show deference and obedience, was one of those norms that would be questioned and partially dismantled in the 1960s and after. What all the social changes of the era had in common was a rebellion against the hierarchies of the status quo and the legitimacy of authorities. Public awareness of the dangers of nuclear fallout and pesticides eroded trust in government, industry, and the scientists who worked for these institutions.

The civil rights movement put on display the governors, sheriffs, and police committed to violating human and civil rights, violently abusing protestors, and in many cases covering up crimes or refusing to hold even murderers accountable across the South. Subsequent antiracist movements have continued to expose unequal protection under the law and police brutality, all the way into the present with Black Lives Matter. The women's movement began exposing degradation, discrimination, and sexual and gender violence in ways that undermined the legitimacy of patriarchy (and laid the groundwork for children, also, to come forward about abuse, sexual and otherwise).

Liberation is contagious, and the Black civil rights movement inspired Latino, Asian American, and Indigenous rights movements. Native American rights activists, who had never stopped campaigning for their land and their rights, pointed out the genocide, the broken treaties, the violations of rights, the unequal treatment meted out to their people. Organizing for rights for and by gay men and lesbians began in the 1950s in San Francisco, Los Angeles, Chicago, and New York City, gaining momentum in the late 1960s and 1970s. After the Stonewall riots against police persecution in New York City in the summer of 1969, something shifted, more LGBTQ radical liberation and rights groups were founded, and they proliferated across the nation and the world. The first Pride marches came in 1970 in a few American cities and in 1971 in cities across North America and Europe, including London, Berlin, and Stockholm.

One beginning of what's often called second wave feminism was the rebellion by young women against their subordinate role in two national activist organizations—SNCC (the Student Nonviolent Coordinating Committee) and SDS (Students for a Democratic Society)—that were campaigning for civil rights and democracy in public while squelching them for women in private. (The antinuclear and antiwar group Women Strike for Peace was founded in 1961 by women who'd been marginalized in male-led organizations focusing on those issues.) "Consider why it is in SNCC that women who are competent, qualified and experienced, are automatically assigned to the 'female' kinds of jobs such as: typing, desk work, telephone work, filing, library work, cooking and the assistant kind of administrative work but rarely the 'executive' kind," wrote the anonymous rebels at SNCC. Casey Hayden and Mary King of SDS declared, "Many people who are very hip to the implications of the racial caste system, even people in the movement, don't seem to be able to see the sexual caste system and if the question is raised they respond with: 'That's the way it's supposed to be. There are biological differences.'"

The social revolutions of the 1960s insisted on other points of view as valuable, legitimate, and deserving and urged other people to try to see from those perspectives (including via alternative spiritual and cultural practices). And, to use a phrase that became popular, the resonance of which may be hard to understand now, to "question authority." We do not accept the right to command or the obligation to obey the way we once did (though, of course, the authoritarian backlash is frantic to return us to the baseline described). But what's most striking and least noted about this old world I've tried to describe is how cruel it was, how much its appearance of smooth functioning relied on suppression, repression, and outright oppression, on the silencing of challenges to that hierarchy and the status quo.

One of the things that happens when a society becomes more equal is that those who've traditionally been subordinated, silenced, excluded, or devalued become audible, and the stories they tell may further incriminate those who were in power. The civil rights movement harnessed this to make the brutality of Jim Crow and segregation an international story, and the defenders of inequality supplied imagery and evidence to these campaigns by assaulting, spitting on, rioting against, imprisoning, and injuring Black activists and white allies in public and sometimes murdering them in private. Feminism, likewise, exposed gender violence, including rape and domestic violence as well as workplace sexual harassment. Indigenous rights movements exposed systemic violence, dispossession, and deprivation of rights, and farmworkers' movements exposed workplace brutalities and exploitation.

Equality means, first of all, equality of voice, means that stories that have been ignored, suppressed, and dismissed might be listened to—if only by others rallying on behalf of that particular oppressed group, though what often begins on the margins and in the shadows of a subculture can and often does gather strength to move out into the wider culture. In fact, a lot of change consists of incubating new ideas or dissenting values and helping them spread and get put into practice as new social relations and laws.

The work of activism is so often to make the invisible visible, the unheard heard, to bring in who and what has been shut out. Often, it's done with the sense that if the broader society hears from the group in question—farmworkers, sweatshop workers, victims of police violence, Indigenous inhabitants of a rainforest under assault—recognition of the ways they've been wronged and empathy for their plight will motivate change. Feminism, over the past sixty years, has led the way on exposing the sexual abuse of the less powerful by the more so, mostly of women and children by men. Those revelations, trickling out horror story by excruciating testimony, one or a handful or dozens at a time, about this pastor or that producer or this politician, made it clear that authority needed to be questioned, that it did not deserve blind trust, that such trust was dangerous.

Which is to say that although the problem was specific both in its nature and in who was impacted, the solution was all-encompassing. It was equality as a society in which everyone had a voice. Because such crimes are perpetrated when some are denied a voice, which is to say are not heard or not believed if they speak up, or they don't speak up because they expect punishment or disbelief or shame and mockery or denial that they and their rights matter. When some are not valued enough to be heard, to be protected by the law, when some people matter more than others. New language around consent had emerged in the 1980s and 1990s and reemerged in the teens of this century, asserting that the absence of a no did not constitute a yes, and addressing coerced and unwanted sex that often crossed over into rape. Again, the subject was sex and power, but the solution was rights and equality.

Perhaps cruelty is nothing more and nothing less than the exercise of inequality as the entitlement to commit harm and the lack of empathy that allows it. Underlying all these categories and all this terminology and all these bits of film history and legal history I've assembled is a secret history of kindness and its absence or opposite. Kindness is central to the values of many societies now in ways it was not then, and its opposite is condemned now as it was not then (even while the revolt against this new culture is—well, one book about it is titled *The Cruelty Is the Point*). Or maybe kindness alone is not the right criterion. There's a moment on a video I saw in 2011 that will forever come back to me as the best summary of what I'm trying to describe: an old woman participating in Occupy Wall Street in lower Manhattan looked straight at the camera and said, "We are fighting for a world in which everyone matters."

If you get all the way to actual equality, you dismantle the old world in which some people matter more than others, and some people don't matter at all. You get or at least try to build a world in which everyone deserves to be respected, to live with dignity, and you seek to dismantle the world in which some people have the right, or believe they do, to subjugate, enslave, humiliate, punish, shut out, and discredit others. Once that's the agenda, how people treat each other becomes subject to different standards, matters in a different way.

Those old movies: what's striking in so many of them is how normal it was to mock and make jokes at the expense of women, queer people, disabled and divergent bodies, nonwhite people, and many others, to find amusement in their humiliation and thwart-edness, with the assumption that the audience—or the audience that mattered—was made up of those who were in none of those categories or who would identify with the people at the top of the hierarchy or would just accept the abuse. The same was true of much stand-up comedy and the kind of jokes cracked in everyday life—and, of course, it never stopped being true in some circles, but those circles are smaller than they once were.

Even when there was no mockery, the films' protagonists often seemed to have a cool self-interest, even or especially in the romantic comedies of the postwar era, in which gender roles were highly prescribed and often played out as ritual combat, and cynicism about the game was the available form of relief. Westerns were often Cold War or colonial narratives celebrating the apotheosis of individualism, and almost always about a rugged, even brutal man pitted against his society, his aloofness, his reserve, his repression signs of his strength. Even when Westerns didn't celebrate the invasion of Indigenous homelands or the conquest of nature, they were about domination and control as key elements of masculinity.

They became so formulaic that Italian directors were able to make, in a burst of what were called "Spaghetti Westerns," even better, crueler, more baroque ones than Americans.

In a different way, the mid-twentieth-century novels I read growing up now seem to have a curious coldness, an aloofness, between characters and a cynicism about human nature. Some of the characters are in love, some of them desire something from others, some have parents, children, or meaningful friendships, but there's a lot of indifference and bystander behavior, a lot of watching people suffer with little to no urge to mitigate that suffering or to assess others by their willingness to do so. It's understandable as the cynicism coming out of the horrors of the Second World War, as alienation from consumer culture, and as modernism's reaction to the sentimentality of Victorian literature.

But, if the epigraph for E. M. Forster's novel about class, compassion, and indifference, *Howard's End* (1910), is "only connect," these books disconnect. In their short history of kindness, psychoanalyst Adam Phillips and historian Barbara Taylor note how Victorian Christianity associated kindness with self-sacrifice and repression, as well as sentimentality, and treated it as a feminine virtue. Neither framing did much for its appeal. Kindness came to be seen as weakness, cruelty as a sign of strength, though there's a case for its being the other way around.

Cruelty is often an act of entitlement—I have the right to control, punish, harm, or annihilate you—tied to inequality. It can also be performative separateness, an assertion that the perpetrator doesn't care about the victim, that they are not connected, that the suffering imposed on the latter doesn't affect the former or makes the former stronger, gives them pleasure and status. The white supremacist lynchings of Black men that became the occasion for picnic gatherings and souvenir photographs have always struck me as celebrations and affirmations of disconnection demonstrated by means of the ability to enjoy oneself in the face of horrific suffering. The same goes for, in more recent times, the videos made of sexual assaults by perpetrators shared around as trophies, boasts, exercises of power and lack of empathy. Cruelty erodes when either the consequences of acts of cruelty are no longer rewarded but punished, or when the sense of separation is replaced by one of connection.

In this light, the revolution in the nature of revolutions, from the 1970s to the 1990s, reflects this move toward a world in which everyone matters. L. A. Kauffman's book *Direct Action: Protest and the Reinvention of American Radicalism* traces how feminist and Quaker ideas were incorporated into direct-action organizing. She tells a genesis story of how, in 1976, eighteen members of the Clamshell Alliance, seeking to stop the Seabrook nuclear power plant, engaged in trespass on the site and got arrested, received substantial news coverage, and came back with 180 people—and still didn't stop that power plant but started the modern antinuclear movement.

Members of the American Friends Service Committee trained them in nonviolent tactics and in the Quaker process of making decisions by consensus. Decision-making and running meetings by consensus seek to democratize activism, to make it inclusive and horizontal rather than hierarchical (and to overcome the charismatic-leader syndrome that had messed up much earlier organizing for radical activists, just as nonviolence as a philosophy and strategy let them exit the largely counterproductive experiments in violence that were also a legacy of the 1960s). Globally, the antinuclear movement became an incubator for new ways of organizing and new ways of relating. Many antinuclear organizations produced strategies and networks and expressed values that had impacts beyond their official goals, including the UK's Greenham

Common Women's Peace Camp, which lasted almost twenty years outside a military base where nuclear weapons were stored, as a major example; others arose in Germany and Kazakhstan.

Kauffman quotes Clamshell Alliance participant Ynestra King, who says that the women's movement had created groups "in which everyone was expected to speak, and everyone was expected to listen respectfully," and, in the Clamshell Alliance, "Certain forms that had been learned from feminism were just naturally introduced into the situation, and a certain ethos of respect, which had been learned from the Quaker tradition." As Kauffman notes, this activist equipment has been used by direct-action movements ever since, including the antinuclear movement, the movement against the US's dirty wars in Central America, many environmental campaigns, ACT UP and other AIDS activist groups, the 1990s anti-globalization movement, and Occupy Wall Street in 2011.

These tactics embody prefigurative politics, the idea that if you embodied in your actions and relationships the values you sought to establish more broadly, you succeeded at the immediate level, whether or not your campaign was successful. It was a practical utopianism you could describe with Peter Lamborn Wilson's 1991 term "temporary autonomous zones." The zones were spaces of freedom from control by the authorities, while prefigurative politics created relationships free of the abuses and inequalities of the dominant culture.

Underlying all this was a desire for radical equality, radical inclusion, radical respect. And maybe kindness. The word *kind* comes from Old English and Old Germanic terms meaning essential nature and kinship or category and then came also to mean affectionate and benevolent; "sympathetic, obliging, considerate," says the *Oxford English Dictionary*. The multiple meanings suggest that we are kind to what is kin. Who is kin to you? To us? Nonviolence is a direct-action tactic, but, as articulated by Gandhi, King, and many others, it is also a set of principles guiding how you interact with others—other people but not necessarily only people, often driven by what in Sanskrit is called *ahimsa*, or non-harm, a word popularized by Gandhi.

Another part of the revolution of our time has been the extension of rights to the nonhuman, notably the rights of animals and the rights of nature. Kindness has manifested in countless ways in many places, as laws governing how farm animals and animals on film sets and in circuses are treated, as prosecution for cruelty to animals, as less tolerance for casual cruelties. Beyond those regulations and legislation has been a shift in consciousness to consider animals companion species, to respect them more, and to relate to them more (and it's also manifested as a rise in vegetarianism and veganism).

Research demonstrating the intelligence and communications systems of dolphins and whales, ravens, crows, magpies, elephants, and many other species has changed our perception of our fellow animals; our own increased sophistication has allowed us to perceive theirs. The bestselling 1995 novel *The Horse Whisperer* and 1998 movie of the same title popularized a now widespread approach to working with horses that focuses on careful observation, understanding, and cooperation rather than brutalizing the creatures into submission. A 2024 story observed of one of these real-life equestrians, Warwick Schiller, that he "has delved into a place where the horse-human relationship is more about cooperation than obedience, more process than product, and where horsemanship is less about a perfectly executed stop or achieving a snappy flying lead change than it is about creating mutual trust and understanding."

The Oakland Zoo led the way in nonviolent techniques for working with captive elephants (most of theirs were rescues from circuses and other places), and I once had the pleasure of seeing them at work early one morning before the zoo opened. When the keeper approached, the elephants came willingly, even eagerly, to be fed and bathed. He was never in the enclosure with them, thereby never at risk, thus never needed to dominate them as had been the tradition in zoos and circuses. He spoke to them in the same quiet voice he spoke to me, saying, "left foot" or otherwise asking the elephant he was working with to cooperate with the bathing by hose he was giving and they were enjoying. They complied, and the whole felt graceful and peaceful.

As the zoo's site describes it, "In 1991, Oakland Zoo pioneered the 'Protected Contact' method in managing captive elephants. Protected Contact means that no human enters the elephant's habitat. Instead, barriers are kept between zookeepers and elephants, and care incorporates persuasion through rewards (positive reinforcement) rather than discipline. On behalf of captive elephants everywhere, Oakland Zoo actively advocated for all zoos to adopt the Protected Contact method for managing elephants thereby abolishing the need to dominate, punish, and use bullhooks in elephant care."

The scholar Judith Butler, interviewed about their recent book on violence, said, "In my experience, the most powerful argument against violence has been grounded in the notion that, when I do violence to another human being, I also do violence to myself, because my life is bound up with this other life. Most people who are formed within the liberal individualist tradition really understand themselves as bounded creatures who are radically separate from other lives. There are relational perspectives that would challenge that point of departure, and ecological perspectives as well. That model of the individual is comic, in a way, but also lethal." Butler speaks specifically of the human, but many have broadened that sense of nonseparation to include all life.

Martin Luther King Jr. brought relational perspectives with his influential practice of nonviolence and his gospel of love, integration, and a single garment of destiny. Rachel Carson brought ecological perspectives with her portrait of the natural world as not a jumble of isolated objects but a set of interconnecting systems. I believe this kindness and this revolt against hierarchy are themselves inseparable from the vision of interconnection. It emerged from many different directions at once.

6

The Disconnectors

There is so much more to say about this rising recognition of interconnection, but this chapter is a tour—and a detour—through the opposing ideology, because I suspect by now a lot of readers are thinking that the world right now is rife with white supremacy, misogyny, authoritarianism, transphobia, savage hypercapitalism, tragic consumerism, ecocide, and climate denial, and they're not wrong.

Two striking things about the new surge of far-right ideology and activity inadvertently confirm that the changes over the past several decades have been immense and impactful. One is how these brutal politics are a backlash against the vision of interconnection. The other is in how the right sees the many elements—environmentalism, feminism, queer rights, equality, racial justice, and inclusion, even kindness—as related, as part of the same cosmology (or in their terms, agenda)—all part of the new world struggling to be born and sharing some ideological essentials. The dying old world is furious at all of it and lurches into monstrosity in reaction to it. I've often thought our enemies believe in us even when we don't believe in ourselves, and this is confirmation that they believe we've changed the world in consequential ways, and with a coherent vision. They've decried it as "political correctness" and "wokeness," attacked it in every way possible, but they also insist that it's important, influential, all connected, and, as far as they're concerned, far too successful.

Authoritarianism and the ideology of isolation are central to this backlash, and are linked because keeping things in their place and keeping them apart are the same project. In his work on the authoritarian personality, Theodor Adorno attributed these characteristics to it: "support for the *status quo*, resistance to social change, support for conservative values, and business dominance in power relations." Since Adorno wrote, the status quo has been leveled and opened up enough that authoritarians seek not to preserve the present order but to return to a past status quo or the version of it that they imagine or wish had existed.

When facing the backlash against the new world being born, many radicals and progressives find ourselves in the unfamiliar position of defending institutions and the new status quo of expanded rights, inclusion, and awareness. The very term *progressive* comes from the idea that we seek progress, to move things forward, but when we have moved forward enough to secure marriage equality or climate legislation or reproductive rights, we seek to stabilize and preserve—or so I hope.

In the 1930s, Ignazio Silone declared that "fascism was a counter-revolution against a revolution that never took place," and the phrase has often been quoted in the past few years. But this time around, the revolution *has* taken place, or many revolutions have. The backlash seeks a return to hierarchy and segregation, to a world where some people and kinds of people matter more than others, which then legitimizes cruelty and exclusion and oppression to keep them in their place and the minority on top. The backlash is a revolt against more horizontal social forms and against a world in which everyone matters, against treating everyone with respect (not that we've arrived in that world, but we've gotten closer in some ways and places). Against a world in which everyone and *everything* matters, since it's usually also anti-environmental, seeking to open up the natural world to pollution, destruction, and development.

Protecting the environment is cast, by the right, as interference with freedom, since in many right-wing versions, freedom means the freedom to harm, while oppression is defined as loss of that particular freedom. Which clarifies, of course, that freedom is for an elite minority and lack of freedom for the majority. (In this mode of thinking, women's rights are often also cast as a loss of men's freedoms, and women are also seen as a part of nature that men have the right to exploit and control.) This version of freedom is seen as inseparable from independence, and independence in turn is defined as lack of relationship or responsibility to others. It's symbolized by the lone man, the superhero, soldier, cowboy, the Übermensch. By the businessman, who benefitted from his race, his gender, his inherited advantages and access, who considers himself, in two resonant phrases, to be "self-made" and to "not owe anything to anyone," with literal or social indebtedness seen as oppressive obligation and unfreedom.*

The ideology of isolation valorizes and protects the individual freedom of some at the expense of the rest and the whole, sometimes by denying the existence of collectives and networks of relationship, sometimes by dismissing the value of those who lose out when arrangements promote inequality and exclusion. Interdependence is seen as a weakness in those who depend on it (though we all do) or as burdensome and stifling for those who imagine they don't.

---

* David Graeber's assertion in *Debt: The First Four Thousand Years*, that money was invented so that transactions could be finished, connections severed, that what we regard negatively as indebtedness can be seen positively as an on-going exchange, a continuing social relationship, that is ultimately mutually beneficial, seems relevant to this desire to owe nothing to anyone.

Independence, as in disconnection, is equated with strength. It denies connection as relationship or interdependence. It also denies connection between things, drawing on the older Western systems in which humans are absolutely separate from animals and nature, men from women, Christians from non-Christians, whites from nonwhites, and on the old stories of lone heroes as leaders, problem solvers, supermen.

The far-right resurgence in this millennium intensifies and doubles down on of the values of elites at a time when they're being questioned, rejected, delegitimized, replaced (and while conservative fears are often dismissed and belittled, they're a meaningful estimate of the real impact of change, and in this, I'd argue, an accurate one). It's an attempt to restore what's being dismantled, to silence the questions, to pretend that the superiority was innate, not the appearance of superiority that comes when only some are allowed education, rank, participation, power, voice, credibility.

Treated as definitive, final, and absolute, categories affirm a reality in which meanings are fixed, definitions are airtight, and everything has a place from which it should not budge. Categories are necessary: we think in categories; words are categories (that can be modified by other words). Thoughtfulness requires recognizing that categories are leaky, that anomalies and exceptions abound, that virtually every description falls short of the actuality. But in the ideology of isolation, blur and overlap and uncertainty and ambiguity are intolerable, and categories are the solution to them, and belief in them is dogmatic. Just as authoritarians seek to segregate, police, and patrol people, so they seek to do so for meanings, facts, and truths.

Powerful independent women, like trans and queer people, unsettle a worldview in which men and women exist in airtight categories with fixed roles. Authoritarians deploy categories and hierarchies to assert the absolute separation of men and women and the superiority of the former, often to enforce racial categories and subscribe to sexist and racist notions of essential difference, to oppose same-sex love and gender fluidity as violations of the appropriate behavior of men and women; to see a world stabilized by segregation (after all, what is segregation but forcing people to stay within an assigned category?—"synonym: isolate," says a dictionary). The most common authoritarian arrangement claims these categories are inherent and natural but proves they're not with all the policing done to impose and maintain them and punish those who stray.

Families, too, are to be regulated and defined, those that fit within a conventional category treated as legitimate, those that don't treated as illegitimate, if their existence isn't denied altogether. The right-wing devotion to—or obsession with—the traditional family as a source of support and obligation doesn't contradict the ideology of isolation, since the much harped-upon family ties are also the denial of commitments to anything beyond it. This version of the traditional family is an authoritarian regime in miniature, with the power of husbands over wives and parents over children affirmed, cruelties and abuses denied or justified.

Categories are the antithesis of systems, at least when categories are deployed in service of an antisystemic worldview and of containment by conceptual and literal boundaries. A system is by definition in motion, connecting and circulating, made up of the flow of interactions and exchanges; it is a process of change. Antisystemic thinking denies that anything is connected to anything else, or should be; insists that there are no ties, and if there are, they shouldn't bind us; that individuals are free, with a freedom that means that we are not entrenched in and shaped by systems—ultimately, that the systems themselves do not exist. If there is no such thing as society, then racism and other forms of systemic discrimination do not exist, and, as conservatives regularly assert, circumstances such as poverty are the result of personal failure rather than collective structures.

As tech critic Cory Doctorow writes, "A key aspect of conservative ideology is hyper-individualism, and the rejection of systemic explanations for one's problems: poverty, unwanted pregnancy, abusive workplace situations and worse can all be blamed on 'bad choices'—not systemic factors. . . . If you reject the very idea that problems are systemic, then you have no use for institutions, and institutions are the only effective response to systemic problems. That primes you to reject the unsatisfying answers of science ('If you don't want to get cancer, regulate corporations and cars that dump carcinogens into the environment') in favor of individual solutions."

This ideology suits capitalism's notion that everything can be commodified, including living beings and systems, and all commodities are disposable. (Disposal itself imagines a nowhere, a beyond, that in ecological terms does not exist; an old environmental motto was "You can't throw anything away, because there's no such place as away.") The willingness to do harm comes from a sense of disconnection, both in the emotional and moral sense of indifference and in claims that there are no consequences because nothing is connected to anything else. The antisystemic view of the world often manifests as attacks on real systems—for example, climate denial is at its heart a denial of consequences, of causes and effects. This denial legitimizes continued destruction and opposition to climate regulations and treaties, not least because these are systems and institutions that are at odds with the unlimited individual freedom to harm, legitimized by denying the reality of that harm. At some level, the fact of climate change is offensive to isolationists, since the climate is the great overarching system within which all life on earth exists, and climate science and climate activism both announce that everything we do has consequences because everything is connected.

Industrial agriculture embodies a version of the ideology of isolation that can also serve as a metaphor, since the attempt to extract one success produces many failures. The agriculture that concentrates on wringing one product out of the soil, often while impoverishing and even killing the soil, requires more and more artificial fertilizers to keep it going, and kills everything that isn't the crop through herbicides and pesticides, further depleting the soil, the natural predators of pests, and the surrounding natural world, and often the animals and people who come into contact with the farm and its toxic products. In his 2020 book *English Pastoral: An Inheritance*, farmer James Rebanks writes about the shift in his part of rural northern England from mixed small-scale agriculture to large-scale enterprises that industrialized the production of one or two crops or a single kind of animal.

One result was the transformation of farming from something in which places, creatures, plant communities could thrive long term to something destructive—for example, raising livestock without crops produced masses of manure and no place to put it; raising crops without livestock meant that this source of natural fertilizer had to be replaced by purchased stuff. Rebanks describes how farm laborers' traditional skills and relationships withered, their tasks became "deskilled, boring and dirty—more like repetitive factory work than the skilled 'stocksmanship' or 'field craft' that had gone before. Whereas an earlier generation of workers had long-term employment that allowed for relationships to community and place, "immigrant workers came and went without anyone really knowing their names." While the central business of creating products for market continued, so many other benefits, pleasures, connections, and relationships eroded, impoverishing the place in many ways for all the life found there and for the imaginative, spiritual, and social life of humans. The myriad indirect consequences withered and faded, and when they were not defined they were not defended.

The animals themselves became increasingly alienated from the land. With large-scale dairy herds it made more sense to bring the grass to them than them to the grass, and in the disease-prone conditions of their crowded confinement, they were stabilized with a plethora of antibiotics, wormers, and vaccines. The land itself became impoverished even for its intended purposes, while the nature that had coexisted with farms for centuries began to die off. "In my father's eyes the work, the land, the cows and the people were all being devalued," Rebanks writes. "Traditional farming people were being broken in spirit. A farmer's pride in seeing and judging things carefully was dying out." Wild birds no longer frequented the industrialized farms. They were mowed down by machines too big to navigate around their nests, workers moving too fast to see them, starved of things to eat, deprived of habitat, poisoned by chemical agriculture. Rebanks's book tells a redemptive story of how he turned the land under his care back into a thriving and diverse place for his sheep, for the wild things, many of which returned to the transformed place, and for the land and water. It was both a move forward to a science-based understanding of how natural systems work and backward to the old ways that named and valued the relationships and overall well-being of the system.

A striking feature of the ideology of isolation is its sense of what's usually described as scarcity but maybe should be called poverty. The sense of not having enough to share, of needing to devour all the resources available, which in Rebanks's farm country meant not enough for the waterways and the wild things, for the long-term health of the land, the livestock, or the well-being of the workers. In the case of farmers, economic pressures created by more powerful people and systems drove them to it. People with more money than they could ever lavish on themselves claim that we cannot possibly afford to feed the starving or care for the earth. It's a spiritual and emotional poverty projected as material poverty, a justification for denying others the necessities even when that means creating tremendous social strife, which the ultra-rich can then buy their way out of, the ideology of isolation as actual luxury goods and geographies.

Rebanks's story is about what happens when you believe you can produce a commercial product while forgetting the relationships that sustain it, can pluck out the part and damn the whole. It's about agriculture as a kind of extraction. The term extractivism describes the ideology of taking as much as you can, giving as little as you can, disregarding the wreckage left behind. It's the logic of colonialism and capitalism that arises from having no relationship to a place, at least none that includes a commitment to its continued thriving. It's most obvious in the case of literal extraction, of mining and wholesale logging, but the logic applies to anything that can be exploited in unsustainable or destructive ways, including human beings.

A lot of Indigenous cosmologies are what was once called animist, recognizing agency, rights, and consciousness in rivers, mountains, trees, sometimes seeing them as relations or ancestors. This has been reinforced in recent years by scientific work documenting consciousness and social organization across the living world and by legal work recognizing the rights of nature. But capitalism turns even living beings into dead commodities to be exploited, exchanged, objectified, erased, justified by what could be seen as a tragic estrangement but is affirmed as a liberatory independence. I quoted Judith Butler in the last chapter, saying, "When I do violence to another human being, I also do violence to myself, because my life is bound up with this other life." In the ideology of isolation, lives—human and otherwise—are not bound up with each other.

This worldview has a history, and many have told it in many ways, with the emphasis placed on racism or the role of Christianity or colonialism or patriarchy. One version traces influential early modern European thinkers—Francis Bacon, René Descartes, John Locke, Adam Smith—as its architects, constructing a philosophy that embraced and justified the emergence of anthropocentrism, individualism, the rise of colonialism and extractivism. Historian of science Carolyn Merchant's 1980 book *The Death of Nature: Women, Ecology and the Scientific Revolution* is one version of the argument that a new worldview arose in this era, and that it was profoundly destructive.

Merchant traces a shift from an organic to a mechanistic view of the natural world and the rise of metaphors of domination, writing, "The image of nature that became important in the early modern period was that of a disorderly and chaotic realm to be subdued and controlled." A nature that is already orderly can be collaborated with and respected; a nature seen as chaotic justifies the idea that human beings can and should impose their own order on it. Francis Bacon, she writes, "fashioned a new ethic sanctioning the exploitation of nature," and she draws parallels between his ideas of interrogating nature and the witchcraft trials of the era, and between the ideas of subjugating nature and subjugating women in an increasingly patriarchal society.

Almost forty years later, the theologian and scholar of Old Testament prophets Walter Brueggemann covered much the same ground in a talk, criticizing Bacon, Descartes, Locke, and Smith for contributing to a modern ideology of scarcity "that sets one neighbor against another in competition for the same goods, so that neighbors become threats. And the sequence of scarcity, fear, greed eventuates in a near readiness for violence." He notes, "These pioneers of modernity pushed social theory in an individualizing direction that negated the old traditions of neighborliness. These advocates of modernity were not evil men, but . . . their theories of private reason, private property, and private monetization have been hardened into absolute doctrine." And, he adds, they contributed to the view that "white European males knew the best and knew the most," which, in turn, undergirded colonialism and the arrogance of missionaries. Brueggemann calls this "a recurring narrative of scarcity, fear, greed, and violence in its modern expressions," an ideology of extraction, of commodification of human beings, of the marketplace, of isolation. Merchant might be the first one I heard articulate these critiques of the ideology; Brueggemann is the most recent; there have been many others in between.

The ideology of isolation had a dramatic impact on the Covid-19 pandemic in 2020, when to care for one another was to separate from and protect each other, by social distancing, masking, and then vaccination, and when authoritarians proved particularly bad at responding to the crisis. The pandemic's most essential truth was that we share the air we breathe. We are connected when we are together even by that most essential and constant activity of life. We inhale each other, our bodies forever opening up to other bodies and their microbes. But for right-wingers, isolation, vaccines, and masking were seen as attacks on individual liberty in the name of the collective good, and were therefore unbearably oppressive and the occasion for much fury and even organized protest and violence.

Some simply declined to mask or get vaccinated or avoid crowds and gatherings; others claimed that masks smothered the wearers or were otherwise unbearable, and that the vaccine was dangerous but the disease was not. Many denied or bent the facts to suit their ideologies. One result in the United States was that, while the pandemic initially hit multiracial urban areas in Democratic states hardest, by the time a vaccine was developed and widely deployed, fatalities were far higher in conservative, white-majority parts of the country. People died for their views; others died as a result of those views.

Their denial was a manifestation of the view that truth and fact are themselves commodities you can choose in an open marketplace of realities. Taken to an extreme, the ideology of isolation means that you can have whatever truth, facts, history, science you want, and so it readily slips into solipsism and nihilism. Language is also a system, and authoritarians claim the privilege to make words mean whatever they want or to use them however they want, to deny what was said or what it meant, to disconnect language from what it describes. Authoritarians from Stalin to Trump see the authority of truth and fact, as manifested in history, science, and journalism, as competing with their own power. They seek to corrupt and vanquish them in order to make reality itself something they command.

I don't want to minimize the impact and significance of what I'm describing as a backlash, and I'm against prophecies when they pretend that the future has already been decided or is already knowable. But I wonder if this backlash is a supernova. When some stars die, they don't dwindle at first; they explode in size and release staggering amounts of light and energy. Astrobiologist David Grinspoon remarked to me, "If we didn't know about the inner hidden or less obvious workings of these aging stars they'd appear to us as if they were gaining strength and becoming something larger or more powerful." Instead, it happens because the star is dying, often because it's collapsing under its own gravitational weight. After the supernova, it morphs into a neutron star, a black hole, or cosmic dust. As a science publication puts it, "But this destructive force is also a creator. From the ashes of a dying star are born the building blocks of life: the heavy elements that make up planets, oceans, and even us." Consider this an elaboration on Gramsci's "an old world is dying," or a version of how worlds die.

There are so many ways to undermine the ideology of isolation, the fantasy of autonomy. You who are reading this, like every other human being, did not give birth to yourself or raise yourself through those first few years of absolute dependency; someone gave birth to you, and someone else gave birth to her, and so it goes; human beings emerging from other human beings down the generations and the millennia, so that you're connected both to the long lineage and the long labors. I sometimes imagine that this business of human beings coming from inside other human beings makes each of us a series of Russian dolls within dolls within dolls, thousands upon thousands of them, ancestors whose genes we carry, generations that are links in a long chain stretching back through human history and human evolution and the rise of mammals and all the eons and ages of life. For any one of us to exist, every link in the series of births and bestowal of nurture leading to us was necessary; if a single one were missing, we would not exist.

All those predecessors, one way or another, participated in making the world we inhabit, the one we arrived in that already had language and stories, temples and bridges and libraries, the one that also had human impact as mountains of garbage and garbage on mountains all the way to the top of Everest and pollution and destruction and extinction. It also had songs and dreams and societies for the protection of this river and those children. And for the protection of California condors, which almost went extinct by the 1980s, when there were only twenty-seven left on earth. They were, through extraordinary dedication and expertise, brought back from the brink, bred entirely and then partially in captivity, the new members of the species released into the wild, so that, as of 2026, there are now almost six hundred, some of them only recently returned to the Klamath Basin of northernmost California, where they now soar over rematriated Native land on wings that span three meters.

We ourselves are not singular, each of us, but plural, a cooperative community. About half the cells in your body do not have human DNA, and your guts, skin, mouth, and many other parts of you are populated places. These are the strains of bacteria and other microbes crucial to your digestion, immune health, and other functions, and they make of you a plural being, a lurching collective of mutually beneficial entities. If you must imagine yourself as an island, you are a diversely populated island, a place of circulations and comings and goings, host to a party full of guests you cannot see but need. Just as a single tree can be one member of a great forest and itself a host to myriad smaller life forms, to the birds and insects, mosses and lichens, and microscopic organisms in its trunk, branches, and leaves, and the fungi, burrowing insects, and microbes it interacts with in the soil, so we are both members of larger communities and communities in ourselves.

It was always obvious that we are not autonomous or impenetrable. Our eyes are penetrated by light, our ears by the vibrations we call sounds, our noses by the tiny particles we smell and by the air we breathe; our mouths taste what they take in as solids and liquids, as birthday cake or medicine or mescal; our skin senses the touch of a hand or the brush of a branch, the smoothness of a plum or roughness of a plank, as well as heat, cold, wind, humidity.

You could not live for more than a few minutes without taking a breath, and the oxygen your lungs extract from the air you breathe is there because blue-green algae emitted it through photosynthesis all those billions of years ago, and plants continue to make our earth inhabitable by sequestering carbon and emitting oxygen. You could not live for more than a few days without water, so liquid flows in and out of you, in as water that was once clouds, snow, rain, lakes, rivers, oceans, puddles, the fluid of other beings; in fact, you are mostly water, a lake in a skin container, sloshing along with its opinions and its agendas, or rather a network of rivers, streams, and trickles, from the veins and arteries to the capillaries, and all the squishy stuff in between. Your life is sustained by lives; you devour them daily as plants, fungi, and maybe animals, and those beings likewise fed on life. You yourself are not a single garment of destiny but a thread or a stitch in the tapestry.

7

Honey and the Hive

Everything happens at once. *Happens* means a tapestry woven together of many events or maybe a tangle, while *history* means tracing a few threads out of the many. Writing history is often an act of disentangling, of creating the impression of a linear narrative, which sometimes clarifies and sometimes simplifies, and sometimes the simplification becomes a stripping down of context to create the appearance of coherence at the cost of meaning or the full picture or just the inclusion of complexity and uncertainty.

Everything happens at once, and while the familiar version of "the Sixties" lionized a few actors and movements while ignoring others, the decade saw an explosion of human rights activism around the world, decolonization across Asia and Africa, antiwar and antinuclear movements, births of new ideas—and rebirths of very old ones, as Buddhism spread across the Western Hemisphere, and as both a respect for nature and a recognition of our inseparability from it were recovered. In 1960, the first woman head of state was elected, in Sri Lanka; African nations were rapidly freeing themselves from European colonialism; and the Vietnamese Buddhist teacher and antiwar activist Thich Nhat Hanh first arrived in the US, where student protests began in earnest in 1961, as San Francisco State University students protested against the repressive House Un-American Activities Committee, to cite a few of the threads.

The Black civil rights movement proceeded along with and inspired other rights movements, in the US and abroad, including women's, Indigenous, Chicano/Latino, Asian American, gay and lesbian (later, more broadly, LGBTQ), and disability rights movements, and the idea of the rights of nature began to emerge at the end of the decade. Science was not separate from the other movements. In many cases, fresh perspectives allowed fresh discoveries, discoveries that saw beyond the assumptions of the era and that would cumulatively revolutionize the life sciences. Among the countless paradigm shifts, discoveries, inventions, and transformations, a few landmarks and milestones stand out for me. Which is perhaps just a way to say that I'm pulling some threads to braid into my own version of a history here.

On July 17, 1959, during archeological excavations in the Olduvai Gorge in Tanzania, Mary Leakey spotted what turned out to be a crushed hominid skull with huge teeth and jaws and a small cranium with a sagittal crest like a gorilla's. Her husband, Louis Leakey, used the 1.7-million-year-old fossil to fortify the then contested case that human beings evolved in Africa. At the time, racism played a role in the reluctance of some scientists to acknowledge this now substantiated and universally accepted story. The Leakeys were eccentric, sometimes wrong—in the case of this skull, wrong that this was from a direct human ancestor—but they played a role in getting other stuff right. That we were all once African was an idea with political impact, and that wasn't all that would come out of Africa in that decade to change ideas about what it means to be human.

In 1960, Jane Goodall arrived at a Tanzanian nature reserve on the shores of Lake Tanganyika to study chimpanzees in the wild. These creatures, so closely related to human beings, had only been briefly studied in their natural habitat, and observations on them in captivity revealed little about their habits and relationships in the wild. Goodall had met Louis Leakey a few years earlier, and though—or perhaps because—she lacked a university education (but possessed endless patience and a passion for animals), he chose her to pursue an investigation he thought would contribute much to his field and others.

When she arrived in Tanzania, Belgians were fleeing the Belgian Congo as it freed itself from colonial rule—the nation, brutally exploited by the Belgian king and then the Belgian nation, had become independent on June 30 (as did, that August, the Republic of the Congo, along with Cote d'Ivoire, Chad, Benin, Burkina Faso, Gabon, and Niger). Goodall recounts in her memoir, *Through a Window*, how she and her companions helped make two thousand Spam sandwiches for the fleeing colonizers before she arrived at her observation station in the forest on July 14, 1960.

Her careful, patient observations destroyed many assumptions about the differences between human beings and other animals. Destroyed politely, in mild language, backed by solid evidence drawn from her years of patient observation, but nevertheless destroyed. In her memoir, Goodall describes her lack of an academic background as an asset in the form of a lack of indoctrination into the conventions of the scientists of the time: "As I had not had an undergraduate science education I didn't realize that animals were not supposed to have personalities, or to think, or to feel emotions or pain. I had no idea that it would have been more appropriate to assign each of the chimpanzees a number rather than a name when I got to know him or her. I didn't realize that it was not scientific to discuss behaviour in terms of motivation or purpose. And no one had told me that terms such as *childhood* and *adolescence* were uniquely human phases of the life cycle, culturally determined, not to be used when referring to young chimpanzees. Not knowing, I freely made use of all those forbidden terms and concepts in my initial attempt to describe, to the best of my ability, the amazing things I had observed at Gombe."

Early on, Goodall documented that chimps used tools, contrary to the idea that tool use was unique to human beings—that our species was, in a phrase used by scientists at the time, Man the Toolmaker. (Since then, scientists have recognized that many other creatures, including some bird species, use tools.) Louis Leakey wrote to her, "Now we must redefine tool, redefine Man, or accept chimpanzees as humans." She proved that, contrary to previous assumptions, chimpanzees were not vegetarian, and she documented the complexity of their social relationships and dynamics. Goodall thought that language most distinguished us from our close relations among the apes—that language was and is our most powerful tool—yet her work wasn't about the ways we don't resemble other creatures but about the ways we do. She wrote: "Knowing that chimpanzees possess cognitive abilities once thought unique to humans, knowing that they (along with other 'dumb' animals) can reason, feel emotions and pain and fear, we are humbled. We are not, as once we believed, separated from the rest of the animal kingdom by an unbridgeable chasm."

The species that drew in Goodall and were the subject of her disruptive contributions to science were fellow animals, fellow mammals, specifically fellow primates. The American geneticist and biologist Lynn Margulis, who was four years younger than Goodall, focused on bacteria and what they could tell us about the origins of more complex life forms and the dynamics of life on earth. She is (or was; Margulis died at seventy-three, in 2011) one of the under-recognized giants of twentieth-century science. Her contributions began with a paper rejected by fifteen publishers before it finally came out in 1967.

Titled "On the Origin of Mitosing Cells," it argued that complex cells, cells with a nucleus, the kind of cells that make up all plants, animals, and fungi, arose through the merger of two different creatures a couple of billion years after life itself arose on earth. Until that time, the only life on earth was bacterial, single-celled organisms without a nucleus. Somehow, Margulis's theory proposed, two of these one-celled organisms came together and neither devoured nor destroyed each other but became a single organism, incorporating the capacities and genetic material of both.

Complex life was therefore in its origins symbiotic and collaborative—"Even our own cells were communes," geobiologist Martin Brasier wrote of Margulis's descriptions of life. She wasn't the first person to propose something like this, but she was the first to do so when the technologies for studying microscopic life and understanding genetics had made available new evidence for the theory, known as "the endosymbiont hypothesis," and the first to see it published and incorporated into the orthodoxies of biology. But it was widely rejected at first. The evolutionary biologist and polemicist Richard Dawkins, with whom she argued publicly and extensively, declared, "I greatly admire Lynn Margulis's sheer courage and stamina in sticking by the endosymbiosis theory, and carrying it through from being an unorthodoxy to an orthodoxy. This is one of the great achievements of twentieth-century evolutionary biology."

Margulis liked to note that for at least half the time life had existed on earth, it existed as single-celled bacteria, and that zoologists, mycologists, and botanists were studying the kingdoms that came along late in the evolutionary story. Brasier comments that Margulis and Dawkins, who is now more infamous than famous for his book *The Selfish Gene*, had "learned different lessons from the same book of life. One of them saw networks. The other saw hierarchies."

Darwinian evolution, of course, had early on given rise to social Darwinism, which insisted that Darwin's "survival of the fittest" meant savage competition, though Peter Kropotkin summed up Darwin's work as proposing that "the fittest are not the physically strongest, nor the cunningest, but those who learn to combine so as to mutually support each other, strong and weak alike, for the welfare of the community." Nevertheless, the social Darwinists emphasized competition and domination and, by insisting it was natural, inevitable, and universal, produced a pseudo-scientific "everybody does it" justification for capitalism and for the ruthlessness of capitalists and elites. Dawkins wrote in *The Selfish Gene*, "Like successful Chicago gangsters our genes have survived . . . in a highly competitive world. . . . A predominant quality to be expected in a successful gene is ruthless selfishness. We are survival machines—robot vehicles programmed to preserve the selfish molecules known as genes." Margulis disagreed, sometimes vehemently.

She proposed that evolution proceeds through, so to speak, marriages rather than divorces—two species coming together rather than one splitting apart. That theory has remained on the margins, but there are countless ways in which species have come together without merging to form cooperatives, or communes, in Brasier's terms. Margulis pointed to many such examples of symbiosis between species. One she describes is a vividly green flatworm, whose color comes from the algae within it, which photosynthesizes sunlight and produces food for both itself and its host. "Algae and host make a miniature ecosystem swimming in the sun," Margulis writes. "Indeed, these two beings are so intimate that it is difficult, without very high-powered microscopy, to say where the animal ends and the algae begins."

She coined a word widely used now, *holobionts*, to describe how none of us is really a single species but a package that includes the bacteria, fungi, viruses, and other microbes on which we depend for our survival, whether it's the bacteria in animal guts or the reef coral that, like those green flatworms, has formed a symbiotic relationship with photosynthesizing algae, or the trees whose roots exchange resources via the soil's fungal networks. As a pair of scientists put it in 2014, "Animals, therefore, cannot be regarded as individuals by anatomical criteria, but rather as holobionts . . . integrated organisms composed of both host cells and persistent populations of symbionts. Animals and plants are no longer heralded as autonomous entities but rather as biomolecular networks composed of the host plus its associated microbes."

To cite another example, an individual termite is both a member of a tightly integrated colony and a wood eater dependent on a gut bacteria to digest the cellulose it consumes, not autonomous or independent on either scale. That example is given in a remarkable 2012 paper, written by two biologists and a philosopher of science, titled "A Symbiotic View of Life: We Have Never Been Individuals." The authors write, "The discovery of symbiosis throughout the animal kingdom is fundamentally transforming the classical conception of an insular individuality into one in which interactive relationships among species blurs the boundaries of the organism and obscures the notion of essential identity."

In the nineteenth and much of the twentieth century, bacteria were largely portrayed as infectious and unhealthy. (The idea that you should aspire to and can achieve a germ-free body and environment is still mobilized to sell products from shirts to soaps.) Margulis saw it differently, and, after viewing the TV show *Star Trek*, commented acerbically that she "was struck by its silliness. The lack of plants, the machinate landscape, and in the starship, the lack of all nonhuman life-forms seemed bizarre. Humans, if someday they trek in giant spaceships to other planets, will not be alone. In space as on earth, the elements of life, carbon, oxygen, nitrogen, sulfur, and phosphorus and a few others, must recycle. This recycling is no suburban luxury; it is a principle of life from which no technology can deliver us."

Having contributed hugely to how we would understand life in its smallest unit, the cell, she went on to theorize life in its largest expression, collaborating with James Lovelock on the Gaia hypothesis that the planet Earth can be understood as a single self-regulating system. Lovelock, she writes in her book *Symbiotic Planet*, "pointed out that our planetary environment is homeostatic. Just as our bodies, like those of all mammals, maintain a relatively stable internal temperature despite changing conditions, the earth system keeps its temperature and atmospheric composition stable."

That is, the earth is a grand self-regulating system that modulates the gases in the atmosphere to stabilize temperatures—until human beings in the industrial age emitted so much carbon dioxide and other greenhouse gases that we destabilized the climate. Because of some of Lovelock's early language and his use of the earth goddess Gaia's name, his theory was sometimes disparaged on the grounds he'd said the planet was alive. What he had really said was that it was a system sustained and stabilized by the whole of living organisms and inorganic systems.

The stories we tell about what nature is are the stories we tell about who we are or should be. Nature is treated as a touchstone for what is genuine; *natural* used as a term for what is authentic, legitimate, proper. This is often twisted and manipulated to insist that whites are superior to nonwhites, males to females, or that only conventional gender roles or heterosexuality are natural—though nature supplies a wonderland of varieties of social arrangements, reproductive strategies, erotic behaviors (including plenty of same-sex pleasure), and sexes (many more than two—including a fungus said to have more than 23,000 sexes—as well as species that morph from one sex to another or are hermaphroditic). Likewise, the old stories of social Darwinism and selfish genes were often used to justify callousness and capitalism, though more recent scientific work has explored the empathy inherent to babies and toddlers and the natural systems that work on principles more like socialist cooperation than capitalist competition.

While Margulis and Goodall were at work in the 1960s, not a few popularizers of the science of human evolution and anatomy came up with just-so stories about Man the Hunter that ignored or dismissed Woman the Gatherer (and dodged the fact that in surviving hunter-gatherer societies, the boundaries are often blurry—and, outside the Arctic, gathering usually supplies more reliable calories than hunting). In these stories, popularized in bestselling paperbacks, women were physically inferior, evolutionarily backward, and dependent on males hauling home meat because women were incapacitated by infants and toddlers—this last part because the men who told these stories also assumed that the nuclear family went back to prehuman history and child-raising happened in small family units, not extended families, bands, or tribes, so the primordial suburban mom was left at home with the kids waiting for dad the provider.

Likewise, earlier scientists justified racism via unscientific arguments for the inferiority of nonwhite peoples. Harvard's zoology and geology professor Louis Agassiz (1807–1873) tried to justify slavery in the US by proposing that Black people were a separate and inferior species. Capitalism and competition, war and violence, were also justified by claims they were natural and inherent in the species. Swedish journalist Katrine Marcal points out in her book *Who Cooked Adam Smith's Dinner* that the eighteenth-century Scottish economist Adam Smith theorized the inevitability of capitalism by ignoring the unpaid labor of women, including his own mother, who tended to his needs into her old age—he outlived her by only two years. "It is not from the benevolence of the butcher, the brewer, or the baker," Smith wrote, "that we expect our dinner, but from their regard for their self-interest." However, Marcal notes, someone cooked and served and cleaned up after that dinner, and that work might be unpaid women's work, seen in the best light as the mutual aid of a loving family.

Garrett Hardin's hugely (and unfortunately) impactful 1968 essay "The Tragedy of the Commons" claimed that because human beings are selfish, and each individual seeks his own aggrandizement, cooperatively owned resources don't work. Of course, they had worked well for millennia, and the enclosure acts stripping British peasants of common land and British wanderers of rights of way produced revolts throughout the centuries into the present. In other traditional societies, cooperative ownership or the lack of an idea of ownership of land also worked well.

In 2009, Elinor Ostrom became the first woman to win the Nobel Prize in economics for demonstrating, in essence, that Hardin was wrong. As the Nobel Committee put it, she did so "by conducting field studies on how people in small, local communities manage shared natural resources, such as pastures, fishing waters, and forests. She showed that when natural resources are jointly used by their users, in time, rules are established for how these are to be cared for and used in a way that is both economically and ecologically sustainable."

Hardin followed "The Tragedy of the Commons" in 1974 with "Lifeboat Ethics: The Case Against Helping the Poor," comparing nations and even the earth to a spaceship or a lifeboat with room for only so many: "We must recognize the limited capacity of any lifeboat. For example, a nation's land has a limited capacity to support a population and as the current energy crisis has shown us, in some ways we have already exceeded the carrying capacity of our land." But we haven't. On the national and global scale, we have no absolute shortages, only distribution problems and a lot of waste, from uneaten food to unused second homes.

There is enough for everyone, but out of that spiritual poverty arose corrupted distribution systems, creating those who have not enough and those who have too much. Hardin's work was aligned with Paul and Anne Ehrlich's *The Population Bomb*, a 1968 bestseller prophesying impending mass starvation because of what was described as overpopulation. The book focused on the birth rate of people in the Global South rather than the consumption habits of people in the Global North, and failed to foresee that birth rates were already falling across most of the planet and would continue to fall, so much so that many parts of the world now have below-replacement birth rates. But the overpopulation panic led to brutal interventions among the poor in the Global South as pressure to use birth control or accept sterilization or even forced sterilization. Meanwhile, the global food supply increased, and hunger actually decreased worldwide, due in part to agricultural improvements.

Perhaps a worldview in which interconnection is a fundamental principle, in which your own thriving depends on the thriving of those people and systems around you, might alter the emotional and spiritual poverty of a worldview driven by notions of scarcity and competition. The ideology of isolation as the ideology of scarcity is self-fulfilling: as free-market capitalism, it creates chaos and desperation, conflict and insecurity, and there is no well-being of the whole to rely upon. A few years ago, the *Guardian* asked me to address billionaires as a climate problem, and I wrote, "One day last year, walking on San Francisco's western edge, overlooking the Pacific, I saw whales spouting, and then I came home and rescued a bee buzzing at my window. The extremely disparate scale of these two wild creatures impressed me and so I did the math: a honeybee weighs about .11 grams and 4,000 bees weigh a pound; a grey whale weighs about 60,000 to 90,000 pounds, meaning that at the lower weight it weighs about as much as a quarter of a billion bees. According to Oxfam, 81 billionaires hold more wealth than the poorest half of all humanity, meaning that in monetary terms eighty-one people are bigger than four billion people. So when it comes to wealth and impact, billionaires are whales and the poor are bees. Except that whales aren't a menace to bees."

Many of these economic theories were premised on the existence of the rational individual, who wasn't really humanity, wasn't us with all our hobbies, eccentricities, and enthusiasms, wasn't babies and their caregivers, but a pared-back version of the pseudo-autonomous adult male under capitalism (or, rather, who has internalized capitalism as an ethos of "give as little and take as much as you can"). Countless examples exist of how traditional cultures took care of the land and established practices and rituals to protect the continued abundance of plants and animals by limiting the time, means, and quantity taken. Not always, not perfectly, but often, creating stable systems, whereas capitalism driven by growth produces instability, most dangerously of all in the natural world.

My own thinking was much impacted by the feminist economists Julie Graham and Katherine Gibson, who, under the name J. K. Gibson-Graham, published work noting that while most of us would say our societies are capitalist, huge quantities of noncapitalist and anticapitalist activities take place every day in most of our lives and communities. They write, "What is usually regarded as 'the economy'—wage labor, market exchange of commodities and capitalist enterprise—comprises but a small subset of the activities by which we produce, exchange and distribute values."

Among these other activities you could list services, favors, gifts, and even presence, attention, and conversation in friendship, family, and social networks, along with membership in religious and other communities, volunteerism, activism, charitable donations, environmental stewardship, interspecies relations, and much more. This means that while, technically, we live under capitalism, it's not the only force present; recognizing this means that we can expand the reach and impact of this anticapitalism, rather than assuming we live entirely under capitalism and can resist only by entirely overthrowing it.

Scientists who emphasized cooperation as key to survival go back at least as far as Peter Kropotkin, the anarchist revolutionary and astute naturalist whose 1902 book *Mutual Aid: A Factor of Evolution* is still a valuable overview of human and animal communities. Kropotkin reached his conclusions in part from years spent in Siberia and northern Asia, where he observed among the wild animals little competition for abundant resources but much cooperation to survive the harsh climate. Kropotkin was swimming against the tide of his time, since true symbiosis, true mutual aid, was outside the worldview and therefore the grasp of many nineteenth-century Western scientists.

In the 1860s, when the Swiss botanist Simon Schwendener found that, under a microscope, he could see that lichen was made up of two different species from two different kingdoms, a fungus and an algae, his breakthrough was widely rejected by scientists, who were attached to the idea that each species was distinct, separate, autonomous. Schwendener himself seemed unable to imagine the coexistence of two species without a hierarchy, so he cast them as a master fungus and an enslaved algae, or as colonial dominance of the one by the other. We now know that lichens are emblematic symbiotic entities (and that in many cases they're amalgamations of three, not two, organisms), neither hierarchical nor exploitative, but somehow this egalitarian mutuality was inconceivable for the scientific imagination then.

Similarly, in the Western tradition that began with Aristotle, beehives were believed to be a kind of monarchy, and the one bee larger than all the rest described as a male king. In 1609, the English beekeeper Charles Butler published a book titled *The Feminine Monarchie, or the History of Bees* in which he recognized that this larger bee was not male but female—some think the fact he'd spent much of his life during the reign of Queen Elizabeth I helped—but he still assumed that it was a hierarchy with top-down governance, as have many others since when discussing hive interactions.

It's now recognized that honeybees make decisions as equals, dancing their proposals for the group until they reach consensus. Thomas Seeley, a biologist specializing in bee behavior, who titled one of his books *Honeybee Democracy*, writes, "Every year, faced with the life-or-death problem of choosing a new home, honeybees stake everything on a process that includes collective fact-finding, vigorous debate, and consensus building. It is a democratic process that humans—especially office drones—might do well to emulate." He adds, "The scout bees have no dominating leader and so can take a broad and deep look at their options."

When the story told about bees suggests their harmony and productivity is the result of monarchy, or colonialism, or even slavery, it naturalizes a human political arrangement, and, of course, when hives are instead described as democracies or cooperatives, it offers a different argument about what's natural. Science has always been political, its ideas shaped by cultural values and patterns of perception and then put to work to support those values and perceptions.

Margulis had used language that approaches a manifesto when she wrote, "Life is not merely a murderous game in which cheating and killing ensure the injection of the rogue's genes into the next generation, but it is also a symbiotic, cooperative venture in which partners triumph. . . . We can rescue for ourselves some of our old evolutionary grandeur when we recognize our species not as lords but as partners: we are in mute, incontrovertible partnership with the photosynthetic organisms that feed us, the gas producers that provide oxygen, and the heterotrophic bacteria and fungi that remove and convert our waste. No political will or technological advance can dissolve that partnership."

Nothing, as Margulis noted, could dissolve that partnership, but the science that once dismissed or failed to recognize it has increasingly come to describe it and even celebrate it. Perhaps the best-known example is Suzanne Simard's decades of fieldwork on forests that she summarized in her 2021 book *Finding the Mother Tree*. Simard, who was born the year Goodall started her fieldwork on chimpanzees, started out in the British Columbia forest industry. Her job was to figure out why new seedlings planted in logged-over areas so often failed. Logging companies wanted timber production to be like industrial crop production, so, after they clearcut the diversity of old-growth forests, they routinely planted monocultures of trees useful for timber. Other trees and plants were seen as competitors for resources, as superfluous interlopers.

Margaret Thatcher famously said, "There is no such thing as society," and, in this worldview, there was no such thing as a forest, only individual trees competing with other trees to grab enough resources. If that were true, monoculture should eliminate competition, allowing more growth (thereby increasing profit). In practice, the trees in monoculture, if they didn't fail as seedlings, were often sickly and susceptible to infestation and disease, especially if they were planted in soil that lacked the microbial life they needed.

A forest is myriad life forms contributing to each others' survival and growth, even if some of them periodically devour others (and even that devouring helps preserve the whole). A forest is a community, a symbiosis, a society, almost a symphony of lives. There is such thing as society, even without human beings around. A few years ago, on a visit to Simard's British Columbia, I wandered through forests in which sunlight filtered through green canopies onto mosses and ferns and shrubs, and trees grew on the crumbling remains of fallen trees also being devoured by insects, mosses, lichens, and smaller plants. Such fallen trees were everywhere, in various stages of decay, sometimes with saplings wrapping their roots around them or shooting up through their fissures; sometimes with mature trees standing upright on the horizontal form of what had once been an even grander tree.

I was at a Buddhist retreat for climate activists, led by Thich Nhat Hanh's senior leadership the year after his death, and every morning I walked to meetings through what I came to think of as the path through the garden of life and death. The generative and entropic energies of forests and the inseparability of the two—or three: birth, death, and reincarnation into other life—are present in every forest, but in the damp abundance of this one, the intertwined processes of coming into being and disintegrating were more flamboyant than in even the redwood forests of my region.

When Simard's research outran what the industry was willing to sponsor, she went into academia and continued looking for answers to her questions. In 1997, almost a quarter century before her book for general readers, she summarized her work up to that point in a landmark paper in the journal *Nature*, titled "Net Transfer of Carbon Between Ectomycorrhizal Tree Species in the Field." *Ectomycorrhizal* comes from the Greek words for fungi (*mykos*) and for root (*riza*); it means the symbiosis between trees and fungi.

Simard was exploring interspecies symbiosis in the forest, in which tree roots interacted with fungal networks in the soil to circulate resources in cooperative communities.

The fungi feed off sugars the trees made out of sunlight, water, and carbon dioxide via photosynthesis; the trees obtain vital elements such as nitrogen and phosphorus the fungi have collected from the dark, subterranean world they inhabit. A while back, this underground system was dubbed "the wood wide web," and it is not only a system of exchange between plants and fungi, but one that also allows trees to share resources between each other, even across species. Simard found that birch trees, regarded as unwelcome intruders and useless weeds by the timber industry, were vital to the well-being of the conifers prized for their lumber, and fungi vital to the whole. You can't say that plants cooperate without saying they communicate, and Simard does say that, too.*

Or, as she put it, "Ecosystems are so similar to human societies—they're built on relationships. The stronger those are, the more resilient the system. . . . We can think of an ecosystem of wolves, caribou, trees, and fungi creating biodiversity just as an orchestra of woodwind, brass, percussion, and string musicians assemble into a symphony." They build cohesiveness, exchange, complexity. "They are complex. Self-organizing. They have the hallmarks of intelligence. Recognizing that forest ecosystems, like societies, have these elements of intelligence helps us leave behind old notions that they are inert, simple, linear, and predictable."

I write this as the president of the United States and his

---

* Since Simard's book came out, books such as Zoë Schlanger's *The Light Eaters: How the Unseen World of Plant Intelligence Offers a New Understanding of Life on Earth* have gone even further in exploring the subject of plant sentience and communication.

henchmen lead attacks against DEI, the acronym for diversity, equity, and inclusion, treating diversity as a threat to their ideal of hegemonic monoculture, imagining, as Simard's logging companies did, that we are competing for scarce resources, rather than that together we can make resources more abundant.

Metaphors are malleable and usually political, and diversity is now recognized as essential to the health of ecosystems. The biologist C. Brandon Ogbunu declared, in 2024, "Modern breakthroughs in biology are producing a picture of life that is increasingly incompatible with authoritarian preferences for neat boxes that dictate what people are and how they should behave. Consequently, biologists must shed the naive belief that our work is apolitical and recognize that the recent attacks on how to teach U.S. history are a battle in a larger war on ideas that includes the natural sciences."

Simard writes, "In making the mycorrhizal-network map, I thought we might see a few links. Instead we found a tapestry."

8

The River Widens

Milestones used to be literal markers, back when land travel was by foot or horse and a mile was a significant distance, and now they're mostly a metaphor for the culmination of something, a moment of arrival, a completion. Milestones have often been, for me, the occasion when progress so incremental I hardly noticed it adds up to something recognizable, though maybe it's more accurate to say they're moments when I recognize the cumulative change, when I notice we have traveled a distance. Asian and Indigenous American cultures and values have become, in recent decades, far more powerful parts of the amalgamation that is American and, more broadly, Western culture. There are milestones, but it has mostly happened in increments and subtle shifts.

I ran across one in 2011, when I was a visiting writer at the University of Wyoming, and the students and I and a couple of cartographers were making, in essays and maps, an atlas of Laramie. A student named LuLing Osofsky told me she missed the places in Asia where she'd been living before she came to this place she hadn't been much interested in. What if, I asked her, she mapped the presence of Asia in this little Western college town?

She did that brilliantly, mapping Japanese, Thai, Korean, and Chinese restaurants, yoga and martial arts businesses, nail salons staffed by immigrants from Asia, a homewares store named Zen Central, and a plethora of businesses, including Walmart, whose products were primarily made in China, as well as an on-campus Chinese New Year's celebration and other social events and spaces. Seeing all this information gathered together startled me into realizing how Asia had become far more present in the West as practices and ideas and cultures (and cuisines), reaching far beyond the people who'd actually emigrated or descended from immigrants from Asia (and, of course, the Asian American population in the US had increased manyfold over the past sixty years, going from less than a million in 1960 to 24 million by 2020).*

In 2022, when the Vietnamese Zen Buddhist teacher Thich Nhat Hanh died, I ran into another milestone when I noticed the reaction of many people who probably wouldn't think of themselves as Buddhists but who'd been touched or influenced by his teachings on compassion, interconnection, and meditation, who had read or listened to him or attended a retreat or cherished an idea they got from him or the idea of him. Buddhism had, since the 1950s, come to have an increasing influence in the Western world, as Asian and then Western teachers brought its ideas and practices here, and a number of writers published successful books on the subject. Transcendental meditation, drawing from Hindu teachers and traditions and made famous after the Beatles went to India to study with one of its founders in 1968, also spread meditation practices in the West.

When Thich Nhat Hanh died, he had established Plum Village, a large Buddhist monastery in France with ten satellite

---

* The Immigration and Nationality Act of 1965 overturned many of the racial biases encoded in earlier immigration laws, and it has everything to do with the growth of the Asian American population since then. It can be seen, along with the 1964 Civil Rights Act, and the 1965 Voting Rights Act, as one of the era's antiracist achievements.

Buddhist communities around the world, and sold millions of copies of his books in many languages. A strong voice against the US war in Vietnam, he had come to the United States in the early 1960s and helped convince Martin Luther King Jr. to speak out, controversially and influentially, against the war. The first Zen Buddhist monastery in the US was Tassajara Mountain Center, founded by Zen priest Shunryū Suzuki Roshi in 1967 in the mountains of central California. Suzuki Roshi (*roshi* is an honorific meaning teacher) had come to San Francisco in 1959 to serve the Japanese American community but found the young white people flocking to him to learn to meditate more passionate about Zen than his original congregation.

With these enthusiasts and devotees, he founded San Francisco Zen Center, which has ordained hundreds of priests over the decades, many of whom have gone on to teach and found their own Zen centers or communities across the continent and beyond. One source counts sixty daughter centers. A number of prominent writers—including poets Gary Snyder and Jim Harrison, environmental writer Peter Matthiessen, novelists Ruth Ozeki and Maxine Hong Kingston—wove Zen into their writings, and the contemporary poet and novelist Ocean Vuong maintains his family's Vietnamese Buddhist beliefs. Other Asian theologies—including Taoist, Confucian, Hindu, Muslim—are influences and subjects of other writers, but the Buddhist influence seems particularly pervasive.

Like Zen, Tibetan Buddhism has had an impact and established centers around the country (apparently including, since LuLing made her map, two in Laramie). Its most prominent Western teacher is the Nova Scotia–based nun Pema Chödrön, whose bestselling books have reached millions. Exiled Tibetan Buddhist leader the Dalai Lama has likewise exerted huge influence, through books, speeches, and in-person teachings around the world, and in founding and funding projects to explore the connections and agreements between the science of consciousness and Buddhist teachings and practices. (Finding these alignments between traditional knowledge and contemporary science evinces the decline of a kind of science supremacism that ignored other forms of skill and knowledge.) Immigrant communities from Buddhist regions in Asia, from Laos to Korea, brought their practices with them, adding to the myriad versions now practiced in the West.

For many Westerners, Buddhism has served more as a storehouse of ideas and ways of being than a religion, if you think of a religion as something you're either in or not in: a lot of people who might not call themselves Buddhists avail themselves of Buddhist teachings. And a lot of people beyond that have been influenced by these teachings whether or not they noticed the source. The ideas that early on filtered out to the wider world were often a little confused; words like karma and nirvana became catchphrases remote from their original meanings, and an idea of Buddhists as self-absorbed ascetics racing to exit the wheel of birth and death in pursuit of enlightenment took hold. Much Buddhism in the West is in the Mahayana tradition, in which the aspiration is not to escape suffering and reincarnation; practitioners in these traditions can take the bodhisattva vow to keep coming back to participate in the "liberation of all beings."

Mindfulness has nevertheless become a personal well-being industry often isolated, especially in the business world, from the ethical aspects of Buddhism (though I once read of a study concluding that though mindfulness and meditation were offered to workers by their employers to make them more contented and productive, it could nevertheless sometimes make them less willing to cooperate with unscrupulous practices). Buddhism offered ethical principles, psychological theories, and techniques to put those into action for the benefit of numberless beings, not just the self, and sometimes its followers engaged in activism, from feeding the hungry to protesting wars and supporting prisoners.

Siddhartha Gautama is said to have become the Buddha, the awakened one, under a tree 2,500 years ago, and you can imagine his teachings as a seed that sprouted, grew, dropped more seeds that were planted and cultivated in wildly different conditions they adopted. There are many versions, but among the core teachings is the idea of what's often termed in English dependent co-arising, meaning that each entity exists in relationship to all the others. As Buddhist scholar and environmental teacher Joanna Macy put it, "Each and every act is understood to have an effect on the larger web of life. . . . All factors, mental and physical, subsist in a web of mutual causal interaction, with no element or essence held to be immutable or autonomous."

It is a cosmology that recognizes interconnectedness both in how things work and in the moral sense of nonseparation and the obligation to care for the whole, motivated by compassion, with compassion itself arising from the recognition of interconnection. Macy notes, "The perspective of mutual causality brings to view a world where 'everything flows.' To be interdependent and reciprocally affecting is to be in process. In this fluid state of affairs the self is no exception." This vision of fluidity and process is eminently compatible with contemporary science, and the two disciplines have reached a confluence of sorts in the exploration of the human mind through Buddhist theories and practices along with neuroscience and psychology. This work has contributed to new visions of human nature.

* * *

Change often happens so subtly, so slowly, that only a milestone lets you know that it has been taking place all along, lets you see that many small changes add up to a large one. For me, nothing has been more profound or transformative than the change in the recognition of Indigenous peoples in the Americas since the early 1990s. So far as I can see, a new era began around the 1992 quincentennial of Columbus's arrival. Intended by some nations and powerful players as a celebration of Columbus's arrival in the Caribbean in 1492 and all that represented, Indigenous communities and allied historians and organizers throughout the Americas pushed back. At the time, Indigenous organizer Winona LaDuke noted that the US, Spain, and thirty-one other countries intended to hold enormous celebrations of the anniversary. She wrote, "It is in the face of this celebration of genocide that thousands of indigenous peoples are organizing to commemorate their resistance, and to bring to a close the 500-year-long chapter of the invasion."

The big celebrations mostly fizzled. The anniversary instead became an occasion to insist that Columbus launched an era of invasion, dispossession, and genocide. The slogan "500 years of resistance" became a widely heard part of the response, and somehow space opened up—was opened up—to discuss what the invasions and colonizations of the Americas meant for those who were already here, and for them to assert, in another widely heard phrase, "We are still here." In the wake of this upheaval, I saw shifts in how national parks and public signage represented the history of North America, changes in place names, in how history was taught and talked about—all things that educated non-Indigenous audiences, while Indigenous communities reclaimed land, language, culture, ceremony, governmental recognition. "After all the hoopla and celebration by the colonial governments are over, the Native voice will prevail," prophesied LaDuke.

A 1992 manifesto for the next five hundred years, authored by a hundred Native North Americans gathered at Taos Pueblo in New Mexico, declared, "We, the Indigenous Peoples of this red quarter of Mother Earth, have survived 500 years of genocide, ethnocide, ecocide, racism, oppression, colonization and christianization. These excesses of western civilization resulted from contempt for Mother Earth and all our relations; contempt for women, elders, children and Native Peoples; and contempt for a future beyond the present human generation. Despite this, we are here."

Indigenous cultures and communities became visible and influential in the mainstream in a new way, shifting the foundations of non-Natives' understanding of the history of this hemisphere and thereby of nature and culture and maybe human nature. Those struggles against genocide and colonialism, for the preservation of land and land rights, culture, language, and human rights have been well documented in books by Nick Estes, Roxanne Dunbar-Ortiz, Charles Wilkinson, and many others, but, to the best of my knowledge, the broader cultural impact on non-Indigenous culture has not.

I grew up in a nation that had committed representational genocide, one in which Native Americans had been erased as though they never existed or discussed as though they had somehow conveniently disappeared. The town I lived in as a child had had a substantial Coast Miwok presence, and their descendants were still in the region, but that was largely unacknowledged during my time there. Fourth-grade students in California are supposed to learn state history, but my fourth-grade teacher gave the subject short shrift. I remember, however, pulling a California history textbook from a stack in the classroom in seventh grade and reading an account in which the many cultures of Native California were denigrated as digger Indians, so named because they supposedly used sticks to dig up grubs or roots for food.

The Indigenous population of California, before its decimation, consisted of dozens of Native nations and language groups with a wide array of belief systems, cultural practices, and adaptations to the many ecologies of the place, from deep desert to temperate rainforests to high mountains. And though they were devastated by first Spanish and then American colonialism, as violence and destruction of ecologies and displacement, nearly all these peoples are present today. The same is true of the myriad nations across the Americas.

But the culture of my youth routinely treated Native Americans—when it treated them at all—as vanished, faded away, extinct, the violence done to them part of the past, to be regretted but not rectified. This view is still popular; I write in a week in which a social media post citing the words of Waheenee, a Hidatsa woman who died in 1932, saying, "Our Indian life, I know, is gone forever," is getting lots of likes. From James Fenimore Cooper's *The Last of the Mohicans* to *Ishi: the Last of His Tribe* to the famous *End of the Trail* sculpture of a defeated-looking Native man on a defeated-looking horse, white culture mourned Native people on the grounds that they were dead and gone, or inevitably would be, though mourning the living is a menacing form of sympathy.

I remember seeing an exhibition in the 1980s that stated that Mandan people had all perished, shortly before meeting a young Mandan artist who had definitely not, and who came from the reservation where the Hidatsa are also still present (and where Gerard Baker, who, in the 1980s and 1990s, played a major role in making the National Park Service recognize and represent Indigenous peoples, hailed from). In the early 1990s, a leader of the Ahwahneechee of Yosemite told me about reading in a museum and then being told to his face that he and his people were extinct.

Extinct or never existed, since natural places were often treated as virginal, untouched, unspoiled, apart from human society, places uninhabited until white people discovered them. Charles C. Mann writes, "As late as 1987 *American History: A Survey*, a standard high school textbook by three well-known historians, described the Americas before Columbus as 'empty of mankind and its works.' The story of Europeans in the New World, the book explained, 'is the story of the creation of a civilization where none existed.'" The environmental movement often described the places it sought to protect as pristine, separate from human beings. The 1964 Wilderness Act encoded this in its language of wilderness as "an area where the earth and its community of life are untrammeled by man, where man himself is a visitor who does not remain," which is at its most basic a mischaracterization of much of the continent, based on what's sometimes called organized forgetting.

Well into the 1980s, white men were still regularly claiming to be the first to set foot in a place, using the language of terra nullius, of no-man's-land, that had justified Europeans' grabbing land across the Americas. (The framing varied from place to place, of course, and in some parts of the American West the contemporary Native presence was impossible to ignore.) Ignoring the role of human beings in the long-term ecology of a place could, and did, result in the mismanagement of it—as one major example, the way Indigenous people used fire as a land management tool. (The regular fires kept forests and grasslands open and prevented the catastrophic fires that result from fuel build-up.) The settler-colonial belief that fire was destructive and unnecessary is now well-known to have ignored both the role of Native people in managing the land with fire and the necessity of fire to the health of many North American places.

All this obliviousness was pervasive at the time, despite the Indigenous activism in the postwar era that steadily achieved gains in tribal rights and alliances. The government campaign to force Native Americans off reservations and into cities had the unexpected result of creating intertribal relationships and identities, which would be crucial to the American Indian Movement (AIM), founded in 1968, and the nineteen-month occupation of Alcatraz Island, launched in 1969 by a group calling itself Indians of All Tribes. A lot of Native American (and, in Canada, First Nations) activism had taken place since the 1950s, recovering land, reviving languages and identities. Books like Kiowa writer M. Scott Momaday's Pulitzer Prize–winning novel *House Made of Dawn* (1968), Lakota historian Vine Deloria Jr.'s *Custer Died for Your Sins: An Indian Manifesto* (1969), and Dee Brown's *Bury My Heart at Wounded Knee* (1970) brought attention to the lives, cultures, and struggles of Indigenous Americans.

But the non-Native population's lack of recognition only really began to be dismantled, so far as I can tell, around and after the quincentennial. From the 1990s onward, the non-Native population of the US increasingly acknowledged the presence, rights, and impact of Native Americans—not everyone, not everywhere, not perfectly. I don't want to sound triumphalist, because there's an immense difference between better than it was and good enough, and because the advances since then have created space for acknowledgment of loss, harm, and trauma—notably, in recent years, the cruelty, sexual abuse, and cultural genocide in the boarding schools to which generations of Native Americans (and Canadian First Nations people) were sent to lose their culture, their religion, their language, and sometimes their lives.

Nevertheless, things changed. No one movement, campaign, book, or speaker accomplished it. There were many things, many revisions of what the official version of American history was and from whose viewpoint it might be told, new signs and names on public lands acknowledging Native presence, new ways of teaching children about the history of their states and nations. Changes build on changes; one shift makes another possible. It was witnessing this transformation that made me confident that culture matters because it can change politics and society, since what began as changing the story ended as regained rights and land, changed land management approaches, and better stories, even a changed society.

In southern Mexico, the Indigenous Zapatista uprising in 1994 was explicitly a revolt against colonialism and genocide. The Zapatistas' new ideas about politics, community, and change, delivered in the poetic manifestos of Subcomandante Marcos and subtle political theory of the leadership, became immensely influential for activists and political theorists around the world. In 1999, Canada created the Indigenous-governed province of Nunavut, an epic reversal from the long era of erasure and dispossession. The new province is slightly smaller than Pakistan but larger than Turkey. In Bolivia, in 2006, after five centuries of domination by Europeans and their descendants, Evo Morales became the first Indigenous president of that country with a huge Indigenous population. The Idle No More movement, founded in 2012 by Canadian First Nations women, spread across the continent. The 2016 Standing Rock reservation protests against the Dakota Access pipeline made many kinds of impact, as part of the climate movement's battles against pipelines, as an unprecedented gathering of Native people from across the continent and beyond, as an education for non-Native people about relationships to the land and the violation of Indigenous land rights, and as a source of pride and confidence for many young Native people.

The old stories insisted we were at the end of the Indigenous story, that somehow the wars and dispossessions and disease had brought an end or at least utter defeat to Native America, or that its cultures must inevitably give way and its people be assimilated into the mainstream, with that mainstream imagined as a triumphalist march of European, white, and Christian civilization. The stories of defeat and disappearance began to be succeeded by ones in which the struggles continued into the present and reached into the future, stories of the beginnings that come after endings. In a recent essay by writer/filmmaker Benjamin Hedin and Indigenous historian Nick Estes, they note that the 1932 book of interviews known as *Black Elk Speaks,* put together by a white writer from conversations with the Lakota spiritual leader and survivor of the 1890 Wounded Knee massacre, ends with the line, "A people's dream died there." But they quote Black Elk from elsewhere in the book: "The tree that was to bloom just faded away, but the roots will stay alive, and we are here to make that tree bloom."

I was hugely influenced in the early 1990s by this new wave of Indigenous cultural and political activism. At his behest, I wrote essays for the Cahuilla artist Lewis deSoto, including for a museum installation reflecting his people's creation myth. It was one of many such stories that came my way at that time. These North American creation myths let me see how the biblical creation story, with its omniscient and punitive god, initial perfection and purity, and fall from grace into cursed ruination shaped my culture, and how differently you could imagine the world if it began with trickster creators arguing and improvising a world that was never perfect, never finished, and never fell from grace. You could. But even—and maybe especially—a lot of people who think they are anti-Christian or anti-religion reiterate the Bible's origin story in which an original purity becomes the irreversible fall from grace.

I was also at the time an antinuclear activist going to the annual spring protests at the Nevada Test Site, where Western Shoshone elders had joined us, because they recognized the place as their land

and the nuclear bombs as destruction and desecration of the land. That led me into two or three years as a volunteer for the Western Shoshone Defense Project (WSDP) in the land rights struggle led by the traditionalist matriarchs Carrie and Mary Dann. Thanks to that work, I had the extraordinarily good fortune to spend a lot of time with Carrie and Mary on their ranch in northwestern Nevada circa 1992 to 1995, listening to their stories, getting to know a little of their land, researching Western Shoshone and Nevada history, witnessing the US government's attacks on them, serving as Carrie's secretary, and organizing with the WSDP. (The Western Shoshone had signed a treaty with the US government in 1863 that did not cede land, which became inconvenient when the Dann sisters forced the government to acknowledge this; in 1979, the courts invented a nineteenth-century date of taking; during the heyday of the WSDP, the Western Shoshone refused to take the money and to agree their land was gone.)

Their story became part of my 1994 book, *Savage Dreams*, about the nuclear wars that weren't supposed to have begun and the Indian wars that were supposed to be over, while they were going on simultaneously in the American West. The second half of that book was about literal and representational genocide in Yosemite National Park. That is, after the initial incursions to massacre and displace the inhabitants of what is now the park, John Muir and conservationists, and then the park service, recast this homeland as a virgin wilderness, despite the fact its people had never left. Much popular representation suggested that the place had been uninhabited until whites arrived in the mid-nineteenth century. Even as I delved into the accounts of the place in the early 1990s, I found books and articles that suggested Yosemite Valley's original inhabitants had vanished in the nineteenth century, but as I researched, the dates got pushed back to the 1920s, or the 1930s, or the 1960s, when the Park Service burned down their last independent village in the valley. Then I found that they had never left the region, and some had managed to remain in worker housing inside the national park.

If you recognize that the Americas were widely inhabited at the time Columbus arrived, you have a history not of discovery but invasion, colonization, and genocide. If you understand the millennia of human presence in places from the Amazon to the Arctic, then you have to relinquish the Eurocentric story in which humanity's only possible relationship to nature is destructive, and in which human beings are separate from the rest of creation.

Stuff like land acknowledgments at the beginning of talks and conferences can seem tritely formulaic and pious, but there's value to reminders that all this was inhabited land, that much of it was never ceded, that the story is unfinished, that Native people are present, and that the thriving natural landscapes Europeans came across in their incursions and explorations were the result of cultures that always impacted, often managed, but rarely devastated their surroundings. That is, you can think about human nature and its relationship to nature in very different ways than most in the dominant culture did before this immense shift. Perhaps in part because of it, another shift took place: Indigenous leadership became an important part of the climate movement, offering both frontlines action in key sites and a vision of truces after the long wars on nature. People who had long been consigned to the past were charting a viable future for all of us. "We're the ancestors of tomorrow," said Madonna Thunder Hawk, an Indigenous rights activist since the 1960s, "so we behave accordingly."

In 2001, I came back to Yosemite for what became a second book about the place, and I stumbled across what felt like another milestone. I had thought that I and the photographers I was working with were there to explore changes in the place since the nineteenth century. But I found that change over the past decade was profound in how the park acknowledged Native presence in the signage (including a bilingual brochure in English and Miwok), in the return to the use of fire as a land-management tool and recognition that the original inhabitants had used it, and in the construction of a ceremonial center by the Southern Sierra Miwuk Nation within the heavily touristed Yosemite Valley. Visitors to the park were far more racially diverse than I remembered, and this diversity made it seem as if we might be entering an era when many stories might coexist and leaving an era in which one story sought to crush and silence another about the place and about its people.

My earlier book had been about wrongness, repression, the need for change, but the story I came across on our several visits convinced me that the change was underway. Again, this did not mean that the struggle was over, victory was at hand, or everything was fine. But things were changing. In 1997, the Museum of Indian Arts and Culture in Santa Fe opened a permanent collection exhibition titled "Here, Now and Always," which felt revolutionary when I first saw it. It made it clear that contemporary Native people had been participants in its creation and were imagined as part of its audience. Earlier such exhibitions usually had treated Native Americans as dwellers in the past, possessed of static cultures, to be discussed by and for a non-Native audience.

Curator Antonio Chavarria, who is Indigenous, from nearby Santa Clara Pueblo, had been part of its creation. A kind man with a soft handshake, he took me on a walk-through of the new version of the exhibition in the summer of 2025 and told me that the 1997 exhibition had come out of, in part, a generational change in museums, as new staff arrived who'd been influenced by the civil rights movement and the 1990 Native American Graves Protection and Repatriation Act. NAGPRA required that the bones of ancestors, ceremonial objects, and works of art held by many institutions were to be returned to their descendants—which, of course, acknowledged that there were rightful owners, and they were here in the present. Chavarria also mentioned the bicentennial of the founding of the United States as prompting peoples of the Southwest to insist there had been other revolts against outside domination, including the Pueblo Revolt of 1680. With that, he took me to see a 1976 Native painting of a priest being hanged, on display near fragments of the church bells that had been taken down and destroyed during that momentous rebellion against Spanish domination in northern New Mexico.

Part of what had seemed so revolutionary in the 1997 exhibition were the warning panels—printed words with recorded voices of contemporary people from different Native cultures advising whether and how to look at the objects on display. It was one of many aspects of the exhibit establishing that Native peoples were present. Along with replicas of traditional Indigenous homes, there was a HUD (Housing and Urban Development) kitchen, which had electricity, political stickers on the refrigerator, and a functioning clock set to the correct time, whose message I read as "We are here, and our time is now." The current version of "Here, Now and Always" has more political context around genocide and conflict, more art by contemporary Native artists, and labels that, rather than calling makers of earlier centuries anonymous or just attributing a work to a culture rather than an individual, describe them as "artist once known." Chavarria noted that what seemed revolutionary to me in 1997 is now a far more widespread way of representing Indigenous peoples of the Americas.

The changes kept coming. One evening around 2010, I was strolling in San Francisco when I looked through the fence on the east side of the cemetery at Mission Dolores, the missionary complex established in 1776 on the territory of the Ramaytush Ohlone. The website for this outpost of the Catholic Church delicately notes that about five thousand Indigenous people are buried in the vicinity—victims of disease, dispossession, coercion, and exploitation, or, to put it more concisely, genocide—though the tombstones mark only European-American graves. Through the bars I saw, to my surprise and delight, an Ohlone hut standing among the graves, a home for the living in the territory of the dead. The hut was skillfully made of reeds, a dome-shaped structure with a doorway, and it or a successor still stands there. It was a quiet, subtle, but powerful statement, an assertion of ongoing presence, maybe a reclaiming of land, and it, too, seemed like a milestone.

Of course, there are so many milestones, so much rematriation of land, so many achievements in the defense not just of nature but a version of nature embodying Indigenous worldviews, and these are just examples, nothing remotely like a comprehensive list. In 2008, Ecuador ratified a new constitution asserting that "Nature, or Pacha Mama, where life is reproduced and occurs, has the right to integral respect for its existence and for the maintenance and regeneration of its life cycles, structure, functions and evolutionary processes." Other countries followed suit in granting rivers and other natural entities rights and personhood, from Canada to New Zealand, as the rights of nature movement spread. This, too, is about the power of Indigenous ideas to shape public life and thought.

In March 2024, after a fourteen-year struggle, the Asociación de Mujeres Huaynakana Kamatahuara Kana—a Kukama women's association, whose president is Mari Luz Canaquiri Murayari—established the rights of the Marañón River in northern Peru, threatened by oil spills killing the fish and sickening those who depend on its waters. While receiving the 2025 Goldman award, Murayari said that the spirits that reside in the waters are their ancestors and the river itself was a living being with rights. Those rights, thanks to her association's work, are now recognized under Peruvian law, and the river has legal personhood.

In late 2024, the climate scientist Ed Carr wrote to me in exhilaration about a major international report he'd participated in creating, declaring, "It is unlike any other environmental assessment that I have seen in that it names things that have largely been at the margins of this sort of work—how capitalism, colonial legacies, and domination are at the heart of the crisis of biodiversity loss and nature's decline. How a very particular version of modernity, shaped by the colonial experience, is a barrier to transformative change because it limits our imaginations, ways of knowing, and communities of practice. How the current structure and rules of the global financial system incentivize disastrous behavior toward nature, and how our institutions do not map to the speed or geography of the biodiversity we hope to save. There is a chapter on visions of a just, sustainable future drawn from a huge number of sources including indigenous knowledge."

In the report Carr sent me, by the Intergovernmental Science-Policy Platform on Biodiversity and Ecosystem Services, a global coalition of scientists, I read, "Currently dominant configurations of views, structures and practices perpetuate and reinforce these underlying causes of biodiversity loss and nature's decline. At the same time, many Indigenous Peoples and local communities around the world have views, structures, and practices aligned with generating a just and sustainable world. Transformative change is necessary to achieve the 2050 Vision for Biodiversity and related global sustainability objectives by shifting views, structures and practices in ways that target and address these underlying causes." The Indigenous cultures despised as primitive, dirty, and defeated in my youth were being looked to for guidance and models to get us to a viable future.

Inconceivable only a few decades earlier, it was an astonishing change that took place mostly in millimeters, not miles, but they added up.

Indigenous worldviews of nonseparation and coexistence have offered an alternative to the alienations built into industrial society and the monotheistic religions that insisted on our estrangement from (and superiority to) the rest of nature. They offer a worldview in which nature is of immeasurable value, is omnipresent, and we are inseparable from it. (Here it is important to distinguish cultural appropriation of the specifics of a given tribe or nation's beliefs and practices from the possibility of seeing the world otherwise.)

The Indigenous scholar Natalie Avalos writes, "In the last few years, Indigenous peoples have reemerged as a critical voice advocating not just for environmental justice, but for an entirely different way of living and being with the world." She describes the foundation of that view: "Native peoples in the Americas understand the universe as alive and sentient. All phenomena in it are understood to be a distinct expression of life force, or spirit. Since all persons—human and other-than-human—such as plants, animals, rivers, winds, and mountains are expressions of spirit, they are understood to be interconnected and contingent. Relatives. The spiritual dimension of the universe is referred to as the spirit world. . . . [T]he people act as stewards of the land, protecting and nurturing the life within it. This reciprocal relationship is mutually self-sustaining."

The huge success of Robin Wall Kimmerer's *Braiding Sweetgrass*, a book about plants uniting the author's traditional Indigenous knowledge and expertise as a scientist, speaks to the appetite for this worldview. It has sold more than 1.6 million copies and been translated into twenty languages, an unusual fate for a small-press book about plants and Indigenous ways of relating to them. Kimmerer has used the book's success to help fund the Center for Native Peoples and the Environment at her public university near Syracuse, New York. She said, at the center's opening, "We find ourselves at an extraordinary moment, when after years of attempted erasure, there is an opening of respect and recognition for Indigenous environmental knowledge. The combined crises of climate change, biodiversity loss and social justice reckoning lend urgency to the moment. At the same time as we recognize the power of the change underway and the imperative of response, we remain committed to the long, patient work of cultural shift grounded in respectful relationship with lands and people."

In their 2021 book *The Dawn of Everything*, anthropologist David Graeber and archeologist David Wengrow argue that Native Americans had a huge influence on European thought. Earlier scholars had credited Native peoples with influencing ideas of democracy, the Constitution, and women's rights within the US, but *The Dawn of Everything* proposed that Indigenous worldviews crossed the Atlantic to Europe. That influence came in part through seventeenth-century Jesuit narratives of their interactions with Huron, Mi'kmaq, Wendat, and other nations of what are now eastern Canada and the northeastern US. Graeber and Wengrow propose that the Enlightenment, conventionally seen as a European phenomenon, arose from the impact of European contact with societies that prized freedom, equality (including gender equality), human rights, inclusion, and peaceful conflict resolution far more than did Europeans of the time.

"In the considered opinion of the Montagnais-Naskapi," they write, "the French were little better than slaves, living in constant terror of their superiors." Graeber and Wengrow argue that this Indigenous influence was far more significant than has previously been estimated, proposing that "most of us simply take it for granted that 'Western' observers, even seventeenth-century ones, are simply an earlier version of ourselves; unlike indigenous Americans, who represent an essentially alien, perhaps even unknowable Other. But in fact, in many ways, the authors of these texts were nothing like us. When it came to questions of personal freedom, the equality of men and women, sexual mores or popular sovereignty—or even, for that matter, theories of depth psychology—indigenous American attitudes are likely to be far closer to the reader's own than seventeenth-century European ones."

It's a deft reversal of the convention in which Europeans spread civilization and impact traveled from east to west, not the other way around. In other words, Indigenous worldviews and values were hugely influential then. I'd argue that they also are now, specifically in a vision of interconnection and nonseparation that a lot of settler colonialists have adopted, or aspired to, yearning for a society in which those values govern how we do things. Or don't do them, when it comes to the destruction of nature, species, places, the climate, through greed, heedlessness, and indifference.

Recognition of our inseparability from nature has grown significantly in recent decades. In the early 1990s, I heard a New York artist say to us on the West Coast, "You don't understand. Nature for us is in the past tense." In those days, I often encountered the view that nature and culture were opposing and more or less equal phenomena, and nature was maybe optional. It was a view in which nature was pristine scenery way out there, not an all-pervasive part of life on earth including the food that became our bodies, the soil it came from, the water we drink, the air we breathe, our own animal selves. The idea that we could separate from nature underlay fantasies of using up Earth and moving on to other planets. Though still cherished by some high-profile tech oligarchs, that interstellar colonizing fantasy is increasingly recognized as impossible (and destructive as well, since it's often used to excuse devastating this planet and regarding it as disposable or replaceable).

Perhaps it has been forgotten how widely people believed in a triumph over nature and over the limits of the planet. It seems now a matricidal dream, a fantasy that we are not bound by—or not embraced by—the larger dance of living things among which we are one of many. Some of this awareness has been brought about by crises, from the pesticides and nuclear fallout of the 1950s to the climate and biodiversity crises now. But that awareness includes not only the bleak vision of what's been damaged. It also includes a vision of the whole and of what could be made whole, and enthusiasm and even reverence for the natural world.

Robin Wall Kimmerer writes that Indigenous language "challenges the fundamental tenets of Western thinking—that humans alone are possessed of rights and all the rest of the living world exists for human use. Those whom my ancestors called relatives were renamed natural resources. In contrast to verb-based Potawatomi, the English language is made up primarily of nouns, somehow appropriate for a culture so obsessed with things. Replacing the aboriginal idea of land as a revered living being with the colonial understanding of land as a warehouse of natural resources was essential to Manifest Destiny, so languages that told a different story were an enemy. Indigenous languages and thought were as much an impediment to land-taking as were the vast herds of buffalo, and so were likewise targeted for extermination."

There's two ways to think about the shift toward a worldview of interconnection and interdependence I've been mapping in this book. One is that it's true, and it's certainly true in many ways scientists have documented, and we can value this worldview as a more accurate and useful view of things. Another way to think about it is to recognize that whether or not it's true, a lot of us *want* it to be true, and that this desire says a lot about who we are right now. A vision of a better way, and a yearning for that way, imagined as the opposite of alienation, estrangement, segregation, disconnection, as the antithesis to the existential loneliness and strife of the worldview compounded of capitalism and the ideology behind privatization, social Darwinism, consumerism, individualism as separateness or selfishness. And an embrace of a better way, as science, as morality, as respect for all life. Maybe this version will fade, but I write in this era and not the next one, and I believe that this vision equips us to prepare for the next one and to leave behind the last one.

The rise of Indigenous influence, the shift in scientific understanding, the return to a view of nature as essential and omnipresent, the move toward more equality and inclusion, brings into focus the change in how we tell the overarching story of the last five hundred years and more. Rather than telling it as the triumph of European and Christian civilization, we increasingly narrate it as one of destruction and division, the result of a worldview driving a society that was tremendously powerful and also tremendously harmful. A worldview that strayed from the knowledge of interconnection, preached a gospel of separation, permitted and pursued the violence of colonialism, genocide, misogyny, and racism, including enslavement; and the violence of extractivism, the destruction of nature, and the extinction of other species.

The novelist Zadie Smith said, in a recent interview, "It's something that I dreamed about all my life, that people who thoughtlessly considered themselves at the center of history, culture, would be made to look at the world another way. That first hierarchical reversal is a revolution in thought, and it's incredible." Because it has been gradual, incremental, subtle, because it has unfolded in many ways, not just one, because it has been adopted by some, rejected by some, it has not been seen as a revolution. But we've seen in this era a revolution in the nature of revolutions or at least a recognition that incremental social change can go deeper and last longer than sudden regime change.

The climate crisis is only the latest breaking point in this history of breakage, but maybe this time around it's not just break as in broken, but as in breaking with the past. Or rather breaking with that past to embrace deeper pasts. What if this civilization was not a pinnacle or a conclusion of cultural evolution, as was asserted again and again for centuries, but a detour from a widely shared understanding? What if that old world was dying, and a new world was struggling to be born—or, rather, an upstart world that had emerged in the sixteenth century or so in Europe was dying, and the new world struggling to be born was the rememberer and heiress of older worlds that better met human and ecological needs, in part by better describing the world? What if this is an end to the idea that those worlds ended or must end or otherwise be consigned to the past? What if our best hope reaches for the future by sinking its roots deep in the past? What futures can we build on these other versions of the past, these other voices with other stories to tell? What beginnings come after such an end?

9

Otherwise

Karl Marx famously said, of modernity, "All that is solid melts into air," as technology, industrialization, and urbanization were fast transforming what in his time must have seemed solid and stable. Marx seemed fond of solidity, but far more recently the Zen-influenced poet Jim Harrison wrote, "I decided we were born to be moving water not ice"—a view in which fluidity and mutability are welcome conditions of life. A new subfield called processual biology looks at the world as made up of processes rather than objects, as phenomena forever flowing and changing and thereby exchanging with each other and changing into each other. It proposes that it is more useful and accurate to think of ourselves and most of what we call things as events.

In a book on the subject, John Dupré and Daniel J. Nicholson write, "The right way to understand the living world at all levels is as a hierarchy of processes rather than of things," and they continue, "organisms have to constantly exchange energy and matter with their surroundings in order to maintain themselves." Life is a constant exchange, a nonstop process of incorporating and producing and excreting; what we call a self is constantly taking in what is not itself, is constantly putting out things—from exhales to novels to infants—that are not itself; it integrates and then disintegrates.

It turns out, in the new science, the new worldviews, we are not nouns: we are verbs.

Of course, Marx was talking about human society and the scientists are talking about biology (and Harrison is talking about worldview), but solidity and stability as ideals can be and have been held up to oppose social change, and many definitions of each of us as individuals attempt to describe a discrete and autonomous being by denying the constant flow—the breaths of air, the gulps of liquid, the bites of solids that keep us going, the more complex exchanges that are sex and reproduction, conversation and mutual aid, society and community, to say nothing of the microorganisms within us we depend on for our most crucial functions, and the other species for other aspects of our survival.

Change is a constant, but social change has sped up in our time, altering the very fundamentals of how we think about ourselves and the natural and social worlds, and also who defines what "we" means. As the imagined barriers came down that separated animals from humans, humans from nature, men from women, that constrained what gender is and what sexual relations should be, that segregated races, that legitimized and enforced hierarchies, some of us welcomed and benefited from a more fluid and open society. Others insisted that without fixed categories and a sort of border patrol around them, chaos had been loosed, and what had spilled out of the containers needed to be stuffed back in. But the changes came anyway.

My generation is a bridge generation, a rider clinging to the back of a runaway horse of change. We were born in the midst of the Black civil rights movement, as decolonization in Africa was gathering force, before the great waves of feminist and queer rights movements were launched, before the environmental movement arose out of the failures and successes of the conservation movement, before the reassertion of Indigenous presence and rights became such a powerful influence on settler-colonialist worldviews, born in an old world that was tolerant of the old cruelties and repressions, the old story in which so many stories were buried and silenced, the old story of domination and control over nature and much else, of the march of a particular kind of "ascent of man" progress that all others had to join or be trampled down or shoved aside, of the constant reinforcement of a minority in authority to whom everyone else was supposed to submit not just because of that power but because it was wielded by men who were supposed to be superior to the rest of us.

There's room for nostalgia about the old world, the world before personal computers and the internet, and its stately pace and rhythm that seem so unhurried now—the intervals in which news as radio programs or TV or newspapers arrived, communication by landline and postal service, delving for information in dictionaries and the library, the heady feeling of leaving the house to step into a world where you were on your own, resourceful in navigating space, maybe with a paper map or just an inner compass and memory, choosing routes, hailing taxis, finding pay phones if communication was needed, keeping appointments and sticking to plans that could not be renegotiated a dozen times en route, the necessity of talking to strangers, of being intrepid in public and present in shared experience that began to be erased by portable cassette players, and then iPods and then smart phones. A classic book of my youth was Baba Ram Dass's *Be Here Now*; tech gave us more and more compelling ways to avoid that.

But I also remember all the oppressions of my youth yet to be named, all the silences around all the abuses, all the inequalities yet to be recognized and denormalized, all the forms of separateness enforced in various ways. Since we don't live at the end of history,

I assume that new light will be shed in more dark corners, new frameworks of what justice and equality should look like will arise. That we are, as ever, in the middle of the story. I have often written about hope—assumed to be how we think about the future, but my hope has come from both the future and the past, and this is a book about the hope to be derived from contemplating the recent past.

The socialist geographer Mike Davis drew hope from that past he lived through and participated in, saying to an interviewer not long before his death at age seventy-six, in 2022, "This seems an age of catastrophe, but it's also an age equipped, in an abstract sense, with all the tools it needs. Utopia is available to us. If, like me, you lived through the civil rights movement, the antiwar movement, you can never discard hope. I've seen social miracles in my life, ones that have stunned me—the courageousness of ordinary people in a struggle."

The radical uncertainty of the future arises from how we're making the future in the present by how we show up, how new ideas amplify and become realities. But it's the past that shows us the possibilities, how the world was changed, how power can appear in places and among peoples assumed to be powerless and irrelevant, how the most foundational things can be transformed, how ideas and arts matter in making the world. As David Graeber reminded us, "The ultimate hidden truth of the world is that it is something we make and could just as easily make differently."

The world changed so gradually that many seem not to have noticed it has changed at all. Fredric Jameson is supposed to have said, "It's easier to imagine the end of the world than the end of capitalism," and most of the science fiction of my youth seemed to find it easier to imagine intergalactic colonialism than women's equality on earth. But others imagined many kinds of equality and fought to make them a reality. In 2024, then–Secretary of the

Interior Deb Haaland said, of her Laguna Pueblo heritage, "When I was a child, my mom didn't teach us Keres, our native language. Her years of punishment for speaking it were too painful. So it's personal to me that our Living Languages Grant program helps Native youth learn their families' sacred languages." Her colleague, former US Secretary of Transportation Pete Buttigieg, who, with his husband Chasten, adopted twins a few years ago, said, "The existence of my family is just one example of something that was literally impossible as recently as twenty-five years ago when an anxious teenager in Indiana wondered if he'd ever find belonging in this world." He added, "That didn't just happen. It was brought about." Brought about through waves of organizing and campaigning, through the arts and legislatures, though countless everyday acts by LGBTQ people to say they were here, and they deserved and demanded rights.

They're both younger than Cleve Jones, who was born in 1954 and wrote in his memoir, "I was born into the last generation of homosexual people who grew up not knowing if there was anyone else on the entire planet who felt the way that we felt. . . . By twelve years old I knew that I needed a plan. The only plan I could imagine was to hide, never reveal my secret, and if discovered, commit suicide." Instead, Cleve became a legendary leader in the struggle for rights for LGBTQ people, and, half a century on, he's not stopping.

After a revolution, after regime change, old statues of the old regime's heroes and rulers come down, names are changed to reflect new heroes, and new values, to change the story through public language and public monuments. In our time, this process has been happening as if there has been a revolution, and perhaps it can be taken as a sign that there has been. Statues of Confederate generals, conquistadors, invaders, and slave owners began being contested and taken down in the 1990s, and the move to decolonize public space gathered momentum, with statues of Captain Cook taken down in Australia and New Zealand, of Cecil Rhodes in Cape Town, South Africa, with the Confederate flag taken down in front of the South Carolina statehouse, first by a young Black activist shimmying up the flagpole, then by decision of the state government. Statues came down despite protests and, in the US South, legislation attempting to protect them, around the world. The process accelerated during the 2020 summer of Black Lives Matter protests, in which statues of King Leopold were taken down in Belgium, a statue of slave trader Edward Colston was thrown into the Bristol Harbor, dozens of Columbus statues and ninety-four Confederate statues came down across the US, statues of John A. Macdonald in Canada were toppled, and others were graffitied and protested. That summer, London Mayor Sadiq Khan set up a commission to scrutinize the city's monuments, and multiple statues of figures tied to colonialism and the slave trade subsequently came down. At the same time, in the US, statues of Underground Railroad leader Harriet Tubman and other heroes of liberation went up, memorials to victims of lynchings were created, and names were changed to create a new public landscape that remembered more people and a truer history.

Almost every public place is what I call a manscape—full of towns, rivers, mountains, roads, buildings, and streets named after men, and statues of historic male figures, mostly white ones; that, too, is changing, with statues in the UK honoring suffragettes such as Millicent Fawcett, writers Virginia Woolf and Mary Wollstonecraft (and three of Agatha Christie) and mathematician Ada Lovelace, and, in the US, recent additions of statues of Sacajawea, Shirley Chisholm, Harriet Tubman, and Phyllis Wheatley have increased representation of nonwhite women. But, since most statues honor politicians and military leaders, roles from which women were largely excluded, the vast majority of statues of historic figures (as opposed to emblematic female figures, such as Liberty and Justice) in many countries are still of men.

In 2016, a Black college student at the University of Virginia, Zyahna Bryant, organized a successful campaign urging the Charlottesville city council to take down a statue of Robert E. Lee, the commander of the Confederate Army, installed in a city park in 1924. In 2017, in opposition to the removal, a suburban army of white men carrying tiki torches, Confederate and Nazi flags, chanting, "Jews will not replace us," invaded Charlottesville, Virginia. Locals rallied to oppose the Unite the Right incursion, and the heavily armed mob turned violent and menacing, and one rioter rammed his car into the crowd of counterprotestors, injuring thirty-five people and killing thirty-two-year-old Heather Heyer.

But, in 2020, the Robert E. Lee statue and its base were covered with Black Lives Matter graffiti, in 2021 it came down, and in 2023 it was melted down after being cut into pieces. The video of the larger-than-life bronze face turning glowing hot as the metalworkers prepare it for the furnace is a riveting symbol of ending. The statue was turned into ingots to be used for a new monument by a group called Swords into Plowshares; a beginning will come after this end. When she wrote about the liquidation of the statue, Erin Thompson, a scholar of public monuments, noted as precedent, "A gilded lead statue of George III was melted down in 1776 to make ammunition for the fight for democracy."

Of course, pushback continues—after the tallest peak in Alaska was officially renamed Mount McKinley in 1970, Alaska, in the 1970s, and then the federal government, in 2015, changed it back to Denali, its Indigenous name. In 2025, the Trump administration insisted on naming it after US President McKinley again, against Alaska's objections, and clearly as an insult to Indigenous

Alaskans. (His administration also sought to restore Confederate place names that had been removed by the previous administration.) I call it pushback, but so much of this could be called rewind or an attempt at it, to drag the present back to the past.

On the fourth anniversary of the January 6, 2021, attack on Congress and on free and fair elections by Trump's minions, Anand Giridharadas published a remarkable essay. He wrote, "I see then that this is both a very dark time and, potentially, a very bright time. It's important to hold these truths together. When I look down at the ground of the present right now, I feel depressed. If I lift my head to the horizon, I see a different picture. This is not the chaos of the beginning of something. This is the chaos of the end of something. And on matters of race and identity, the Trump era doesn't have the crackle of a launch. It has been a mourning. A mourning for white power. A mourning for a time when simply to be white and show up was enough. A mourning for an era in which simply to be a man, and not necessarily an especially capable one, could get you ahead of other people. We must understand that what we've been living through is backlash. Backlash. It's not the engine of history. It is the revolt against the engine of history."

An old world was dying. This is the time of monsters.

But Giridharadas went on: "We are living through a revolt against the future. The future will prevail." A new world is struggling, but it is also being born, or perhaps it has been born and is struggling with its first breaths, its first steps. Arundhati Roy had put it another way in her address to the World Social Forum in 2003: "Another world is not only possible, she's on her way. Maybe many of us won't be here to greet her, but on a quiet day, if I listen very carefully, I can hear her breathing." Of course, worlds are always being born, always being swept away; change is the only constant. But the transformation of everyday life has in recent decades been revolutionary in its scope, its reach into every arena of life, from how we produce energy to how we think about food and nature and human rights.

One thing I've learned through the back-and-forths over the years is that you can take rights away, but you can't so easily take ideas away, including people's belief in their own rights and the rights of people they care about. You can cut down the flowers, but you can't stop the spring. There is no going back, though how we go forward is the work—or conflict—at hand. Giridharadas and I both believe that contemporary right-wing authoritarianism is waging a war against the future, against the world being created and in many ways already well established, through what were once radical ideas of universal human rights and equality, across race and gender, ideas about our inseparability from nature that never died in the margins but were denied in the centers of power. We have won enough that we are in what is to some the unfamiliar position of defending a(n imperfect and incomplete) revolution against backlash and counterrevolution.

I have always drawn my hope from the past, not the future, from the way the past shows us how change works, how what once seemed impossible becomes actuality, from how it models the ways that power works in contradiction to what the officially powerful tell us. I do not know what's to come, and I have avoided prophecy when it pretends the future is foreordained, decided, rather than something that we're making—or competing to make—in the present. I see promising signs—seeds—in how so many young people regard both their own gender and their sexual orientation as fluid or just not something needing definition, in a rising generation used to coexisting with people of other races and religions and origins, in the confidence of young women in their own rights in ways my generation lacked, in the widespread awareness of the real history of the Americas and the presence of Indigenous people and nations, in a growing attachment to the natural world and wild places, in an ethic of kindness toward animals, in a sense that capitalism is both cruel and destructive and there are other, better ways to arrange things.

Those changes, in a sense, are all the harvest from seeds planted long ago. I see new seedlings in the return to the possibility of utopia as Afrofuturism, Indigenous futurism, Latinofuturism, each of which is the refusal to be doomed or marginal; I see it in speculative fiction that dares other versions than the dystopian, in the rise of new forms of media as legacy media continues to fail us, in the recognition of the many disasters Silicon Valley has brought us, from what it's done to our attention and our elections to what it's doing to our climate, in polls showing the widespread support for climate action. Seedlings need tending and watering and maybe weeding of the destructive forces that could outcompete them. We have our work cut out for us. It's good work, and it's everyone's work. Countless people are doing it with whatever love, devotion, and brilliance they bring to the task; it needs more of us and more from us.

You don't need to know the future to act in the present, which is good because you can't. As I revised this book, beloved Buddhist scholar and climate leader Joanna Macy was dying at home across the bay from me, and some of her words came back to me. In 2010, she had said in an interview, "There's a song that wants to sing itself through us, and we've just got to be available. Maybe the song that is to be sung through us is the most beautiful requiem for an irreplaceable planet or maybe it's a song of joyous rebirth as we create a new culture that doesn't destroy its world." We're deciding what it is by what we sing, by what alliances we make, actions we take, possibilities we act on, bridges and refuges we build. And what we dismantle because it does not serve the broader *us* and *we*.

"We are creating a world we have never seen," wrote adrienne maree brown in *Emergent Strategy*. "We are whispering it to each other cuddled in the dark, and we are screaming it at people who are so scared of it that they dress themselves in war regalia to turn and face us." Whether or not they turn to face us, we face the past to remember, we face the future to dream. And we know we live in the dreams, some realized, some defeated, some on their way, of those who came before.

Acknowledgments

This book opens with my journey to, or rather arrival at, the Federated Indians of Graton Rancheria Land Back celebration; what doesn't fit into the first chapter's account is that I had a car tire pressure indicator freaking out about the tire pressure on my brand-new tires, so the journey began early that morning with the infinite generosity and kindness of the Latino guys at the local brake shop who reassured me that the pressure was okay and refused to accept payment. And then, on the drive there, I listened to adrienne maree brown and Autumn Brown's conversation with Black feminist scholar Brittney Cooper, on the sisters' podcast *How to Survive the End of the World*. My life—and yours, I hope—is illuminated and improved by small encounters like that, and my gratitude extends far beyond what I can list. Of course, the sources quoted in the text and cited in the endnotes give some sense of that.

My first gratitude goes to the unceded land of the Coast Miwok on which I grew up, which gave me joy, refuge, and so much to learn and discover; my second, to the unceded territory of the Ramaytush Ohlone, on the other side of the Golden Gate Bridge, where I've spent much of my adult life, walking thousands of miles on its beaches, streets, over its hills, through its parks, and benefiting from its magnificent public library and bookstores. Most of this book was written in San Francisco, with regular excursions across that bridge to wide-open spaces. Thanks much to

Greg Sarris and Angela Hardin of the Federated Tribes of Graton Rancheria, to archeologist Kyle Rabellino, and to Josh Kling of the Western Rivers Conservancy for helping me understand what that place and occasion described in this book's first chapter meant.

But some of this book was conceived and written—and discussed and inspired—at Upaya Zen Center on unceded Tewa territory in northern New Mexico, as a guest of Roshi Joan Halifax, my extraordinary friend who has, in a bit more than eight decades, not only lived through all the changes described in this book but participated in many of them and furthered others, as a civil rights activist, early student of Thich Nhat Hanh, medical anthropologist, feminist, climate activist, explorer of the frontiers of consciousness, Buddhist leader, and principal in the Mind & Life Institute's work of building bridges and tracing relationships between Buddhist teachings and contemporary science, particularly the science of mind. Roshi astonished and delighted me when I was staying with her in November 2024 by mentioning that the room I slept in had been Lynn Margulis's room a few decades back, but she has, over the years of our friendship, done so more by her stories and her brilliance—her ability to synthesize deep and broad knowledge across many fields and to always deploy that knowledge in the service of the greater good.

I've dedicated some of my earlier books to the young people in my life who represent the future to me, the ones who might well be alive in the year 2100. But for this one, I'd like to give a deep bow to those who came before, especially Carrie (1932–2021) and Mary (1923–2005) Dann, whose presence and power were a great education during the years, circa 1992–1995, I was lucky enough to spend a lot of time with them, listen to them, travel their homeland of Newe Sogobia/northeastern Nevada with them, and support them in a land-rights struggle that was ultimately unsuccessful but valiantly fought and that drew in many of us in ways that were transformative.

Carrie and Mary felt like the two most free and unsubjugated women I'd ever met, and it was thanks to Nevada organizer B. Fulkerson and Western Shoshone activist Virginia Sanchez that I connected with them in the first place. That time with these two matriarchs crowned a vast education or reeducation I underwent from the mid-1980s, as I sought to try to understand who and where I was as a resident of the American West, to understand and move beyond the Eurocentric ideas about nature and place that were then ambient, to find ways to think about landscape and the environment, and to become an environmental activist. And a writer.

The present in which I write is a remarkable era, even a golden age. It's also a time of terrible depredations, of course, but also of valiant resistance, not just in practical ways, but in endlessly creative and imaginative rethinking of the values and possibilities, of gorgeous literary work not just for its style but for its vision, scientific discoveries with profound philosophical and social implications and reinforcement of countervailing narratives. I was raised to think of greatness as originality, exceptionalness, individuality, but for me at present, great work makes most sense as part of a collective conversation and reinvention, each individual effort a contribution to the grander project.

This is a book about things that happened only because people showed up, only because people believed the world could be different, only because people became the forces of change, sometimes by joining together, sometimes by chasing down new frameworks and possibilities and telling the world about them, only because people didn't give up when it looked like they were losing, only because they married the wildest idealism to the staunchest pragmatism. I had a wave of gratitude as I was writing these acknowledgments, gratitude for the courage, generosity, and integrity of the people I connect with regularly as a friend, collaborator, fellow climate and democracy activist; for all the people I see and hear and read about doing the work to protect the earth, human rights, democracy, and truth; for all those meeting the crises as they should be met.

Among those I'm grateful to: all the people in the streets at the Tesla Takedown and #NoKings and anti-ICE protests I participated in in 2025, the year people turned out all over the US to stop the attacks on immigrants; Thelma, Daniel, and Sabrina of the Hope Squad; Cleve Jones and all the drag queens for democracy around here; the whole gang at Oil Change International; Bill McKibben and the crew at Third Act; Erik Mebust, Yotam Marom, Julian Aguon, and all the next generation of changemakers who let me hang out with them; Erica, Susan, Brian, Saket, Will, Joe, Red, Marina, Astra, Blake, Terry, Tzeporah, Conchita, Molly, Leah, Antonia, and all the friends whose conversation weaves a web of possibility.

And, once again, my agent Frances Coady and everyone at Haymarket Books and Granta were a joy to work with.

I'm grateful to everyone who refused to surrender in advance. To those who persevered when the future seemed dark, who saw the night as the time in which we dream and grow, who became torches or North Stars when we needed illumination or direction. To all the visionary souls and heroes who made the changes this book tries to describe. To all those making the shifts toward a better world now, the ones just coming into focus or that we'll see clearly in ten or fifty or a hundred years, the ones that make the news and the ones that happen in secret and touch one life or protect one place. To everyone who keeps looking, hoping, working. To those who know that while we can't save everything, everything we can save matters.

Notes

Epigraphs

v "We are caught in an inescapable network of mutuality": Martin Luther King Jr., "Letter from a Birmingham Jail," 1963; slight variation included in "The Man Who Was a Fool," a 1961 sermon published in Martin Luther King Jr., *The Strength to Love* (Fortress Press, 2010), 69.

v "We are living through a revolt against the future. The future will prevail": Anand Giridharadas, "January 6 Was a Revolt Against the Future. The Future Will Prevail: A Reflection, Four Years On," *The Ink*, January 6, 2025.

v "We're the ancestors of tomorrow, so we behave accordingly": Madonna Thunder Hawk, quoted in Nick Estes, *Our History Is the Future: Standing Rock Versus the Dakota Access Pipeline, and the Long Tradition of Indigenous Resistance* (Haymarket Books, 2024), 266.

1. Swimming Upstream

1 "'Hope and history rhyme'": Seamus Heaney, *The Cure at Troy: A Version of Sophocles' Philoctetes* (Faber & Faber, 2018).

2 "'It's amazing,' said Ron Reed, a fisherman from the Karuk tribe": Ian James, "'A Beautiful Thing': Klamath River Salmon Are Spotted Far Upstream in Oregon After Dam Removal," *Los Angeles Times*, October 19, 2024.

2. Winged Seeds

11 "Environmentalist Gus Speth writes that visions of a better world 'will not compete yet in today's practical politics'": Gus Speth, "Odyssey:

Hopes and Dreams," *Resilience*, December 10, 2024, www.resilience.org/stories/2024-12-10/odyssey-hopes-and-dreams/.

13   "[Antonio Gramsci] wrote, around 1930, 'La crisi consiste appunto nel fatto che il vecchio muore e il nuovo non può nascere: in questo interregno si verificano i fenomeni morbosi piú svariati'": provided by translator Andrea Spila.

15   "Amitav Ghosh has another take on the monsters, writing, 'What is distinctive about our time is that its monsters . . .'": Amitav Ghosh, speech, Erasmus Prize, November 26, 2024, transcription at https://scroll.in/article/1076239/amitav-ghosh-in-this-time-of-monstrous-anomalies-we-must-recognise-that-the-earth-is-judging-us.

16   "You can cut down the flowers, but you can't stop the spring": Many attribute this line or the Spanish "Podrán cortar todas las flores, pero no podrán detener la primavera" to Pablo Neruda, but no one cites an actual source from something he said or wrote, and some say there is none.

16   "Thomas Berry wrote, in words echoing Gramsci's, 'We are in trouble because we do not have a good story'": *Teilhard Studies*, no. 1 (Winter 1978); and Thomas Berry, "The New Story," in *Teilhard in the 21st Century: The Emerging Spirit of Earth*, eds. Arthur Fabel and Donald St. John (Orbis Books, 2003), 77–88, https://newstories.org/wp-content/uploads/2024/10/Thomas_Berry-The_New_Story_4340.pdf.

3. Varieties of Invisibility

22   "Bill McKibben wrote in the summer of 2025, 'In the past two years, however . . .'": Bill McKibben, "4.6 Billion Years On, the Sun Is Having a Moment," *New Yorker*, July 9, 2025.

27   "As Jonathan Schell once wrote of how revolutions unfold in the imagination first, 'Individual hearts and minds change'": Jonathan Schell, *The Unconquerable World: Power, Nonviolence, and the Will of the People* (Metropolitan Books, 2003), 166–67.

27   "I've traced with pleasure how British suffragists protesting for the right to vote in London influenced a young Indian lawyer," in the essay "In Praise of Indirect Consequences," in my book *Call Them by Their True Names* (Haymarket, 2018), originally published in the *Guardian*, https://www.theguardian.com/world/2017/mar/13/protest-persist-hope-trump-activism-anti-nuclear-movement.

28   "Zhou Enlai . . . replied, 'Too soon to tell'": The source below and some others insist he was talking about 1968, not 1789, but it's still a meaningful answer, reflecting a long, patient timeline rather than the rush to verdicts as or just after something transpires: *South China Morning Post*, "Not Letting the Facts Ruin a Good Story," June 15, 2011, https://www.scmp.com/article/970657/not-letting-facts-ruin-good-story.

4. A Single Garment of Destiny

31   "'A sample of drinking water from an orchard area in Pennsylvania . . .'": Rachel Carson, *Silent Spring* (Houghton Mifflin Company, 1962), 41.

32   "'None could live in the tiny creek . . .'": Carson, *Silent Spring*, 68.

33   "'The fact that every meal we eat carries its load of chlorinated hydrocarbons is the inevitable consequence . . .'": Carson, *Silent Spring*, 180.

33   "'Can anyone believe it is possible to lay down such a barrage of poisons . . .'": Carson, *Silent Spring*, 7–8.

33   Reintroducing wolves to Yellowstone National Park has been widely documented, including the following sources: Douglas W. Smith, Daniel R. Stahler, Matthew C. Metz, et al., "Wolf Restoration in Yellowstone: Reintroduction to Recovery," *National Park Service*, https://www.nps.gov/articles/wolf-restoration-in-yellowstone-reintroduction-to-recovery.htm; and Andy P. Dobston, "Yellowstone Wolves and the Forces That Structure Natural Systems," *PLoS Biology*, December 23, 2014, https://journals.plos.org/plosbiology/article?id=10.1371/journal.pbio.1002025.

34   "Barry Commoner wrote up 'the four laws of ecology'": Barry Commoner, *The Closing Circle: Nature, Man, and Technology* (Knopf, 1971), 33–46.

34   "Activists, including Women Strike for Peace": Women Strike for Peace is a remarkably significant, remarkably unknown force in antiwar and antinuclear activism, as well as in feminism. I wrote about the group at length in my 1994 book *Savage Dreams*, and Amy Swerdlow's 1993 history of WSP is the best resource on their history and impact. (I'm violating the consistency of these endnotes to make one more plug for the group.)

35   "Martin Luther King Jr. remarked in that period, 'One cannot be concerned just with civil rights. It is very nice to drink milk . . .'": quoted

by Drew Dellinger in "Martin Luther King: Ecological Thinker," *Common Ground*, 2014.

35   "King wrote in his 'Letter from a Birmingham Jail' that 'we are caught in an inescapable network of mutuality . . .'": see first epigraph.

35   "Whole closely knit fabric of life . . .": Carson, *Silent Spring*, 67.

35   "'I can never be what I ought until you are what you ought to be . . .'": Martin Luther King Jr., "The Man Who Was a Fool," 1961 sermon, in *The Strength to Love* (Fortress Press, 2010/1963), 69.

36   "In his book about the 1955 Montgomery Bus Boycott, King wrote that 'Gandhi was probably the first person in history . . .'": Martin Luther King Jr., *Stride Toward Freedom: The Montgomery Story* (Harper & Row, 1958), 91.

36   "'Those of us who lived in the twentieth century are privileged to live in one of the most momentous periods of human history . . .'": Martin Luther King Jr., "The Birth of a New Age," address delivered at the fiftieth anniversary of the founding of Alpha Phi Alpha, August 11, 1956, Buffalo New York, Stanford University Archives, https://kinginstitute.stanford.edu/king-papers/documents/birth-new-age-address-delivered-11-august-1956-fiftieth-anniversary-alpha-phi.

36   "'We live in one world geographically. We face the great problem of making it one spiritually,' he declared": King, "The Birth of a New Age."

36   "Grace Lee Boggs . . . wrote . . . that the bus boycott was 'the first struggle by an oppressed people in Western society from this new philosophical/political perspective' and 'their goal was not only desegregating the buses . . .'": Grace Lee Boggs with Scott Tadeo Kurashige, *The Next American Revolution: Sustainable Activism for the Twenty-First Century* (University of California Press, 2012), 39.

37   "'Men and women who had been separated from each other . . .'": King, *Stride Toward Freedom*, 86.

37   "'Whereas desegregation can be brought about by laws, integration requires a change in attitudes. . . .'": Martin Luther King Jr., quoted in Kenneth L. Smith and Ira G. Zepp Jr., "Martin Luther King's Vision of the Beloved Community," online version adapted from their book *Search for the Beloved Community: The Thinking of Martin Luther King Jr.* (Judson Press, 1974).

38   "[Rosa Parks] was, in fact, a courageous and important organizer with the NAACP": see Danielle L. McGuire, *At the Dark End of the Street:*

Black Women, Rape, and Resistance—A New History of the Civil Rights Movement from Rosa Parks to the Rise of Black Power (Vintage, 2011); and Jeanne Theoharis, *The Rebellious Life of Mrs. Rosa Parks* (Beacon Press, 2012).

39 "He noted, 'The good neighbor looks beyond the external accidents . . .'": King, *The Strength to Love*, 25.

40 "King scholar Drew Dellinger writes, 'As early as the Montgomery Bus Boycott in 1956, King said . . .'": Dellinger, *Common Ground*, 2014.

5. Shadows of the Past

43 "'She no longer hopes to live by seeking the truth . . .'": T. H. White, *The Once and Future King* (G. P. Putnam's Sons, 1938), 367.

45 "Molly Ringwald . . . wrote an essay": Molly Ringwald, "What About *The Breakfast Club*: Revisiting the Movies of My Youth in the Age of #MeToo," *New Yorker*, April 6, 2018.

48 "Gloria Steinem reported in 1969, 'Forty-three states have "protection legislation" limiting the hours . . .'": *New York*, April 11, 1969.

48 "At the University of Virginia in the late nineteenth century, instruction of women was denied on the grounds that education 'does often physically unsex them . . .'": Ed Miller, "It Was About Time: A Timeline of Women at UVA," *UVA Magazine*, Fall 2020, https://uvamagazine.org/articles/timeline_of_women_at_uva.

49 "Rachel Carson, for example, was often described in print as overwrought and incompetent": *Time* magazine's review of *Silent Spring* described her as "hysterically overemphatic," in this "emotional and inaccurate outburst": "Biology: Pesticides: The Price for Progress," *Time*, September 28, 1962, https://time.com/archive/6873182/biology-pesticides-the-price-for-progress/.

49 "'It was idiots, convicts, minors, and married women who didn't have property rights'": Louise Ballerstedt Raggio, cited by State Bar of Texas at https://www.texasbar.com/AM/Template.cfm?Section=Making_the_Case&Template=/CM/HTMLDisplay.cfm&ContentID=14882; Raggio may have been paraphrasing a feminist pamphlet published in Britain in 1868, which noted, "Pardon me; I must seem to you so stupid! Why is the property of the woman who commits Murder, and the property of the woman who commits Matrimony, dealt with alike by your law?"

49   "In 1981, the Supreme Court overturned the last 'head and master' law": see *Kirchberg v. Feenstra*, 450 U.S. 455 (1981).

54   "'Consider why it is in SNCC that women who are competent . . .'": pdf reproduction of the original at https://snccdigital.org/wp-content/uploads/digitalcollections/6411w_us_women.pdf. This and the SDS declaration in the next note are both referenced in Ruth Rosen, *The World Split Open: How the Modern Women's Movement Changed America* (Viking, 2000).

54   "Casey Hayden and Mary King of SDS declared, 'Many people who are very hip to the implications of the racial caste system . . .'": facsimile of the original at https://www.crmvet.org/docs/651118_kind-of_memo.pdf.

60   "Kauffman quotes Clamshell alliance participant Ynestra King, who says that the women's movement had created groups 'in which everyone was expected to speak, and everyone was expected to listen respectfully' and, in the Clamshell Alliance, 'Certain forms that had been learned from feminism . . .'": L. A. Kauffman, *Direct Action: Protest and the Reinvention of American Radicalism* (Verso, 2017), 55.

62   "The scholar Judith Butler . . . said, 'In my experience, the most powerful argument against violence . . .'": Masha Gessen, interview, *New Yorker*, February 9, 2020.

6. The Disconnectors

65   "Theodor Adorno attributed these characteristics to it: 'support for the *status quo*, resistance to social change, support for conservative values, and business dominance in power relations'": cited by D. Robert Worley, "Adorno et al. The Authoritarian Personality 1950," 2021, https://doi.org/10.13140/RG.2.2.17003.26403.

69   "As tech critic Cory Doctorow writes, 'A key aspect of conservative ideology is hyper-individualism'": Cory Doctorow, "Conservatism Considered as a Movement of Bitter Rubes," *Pluralistic*, July 22, 2025, https://pluralistic.net/2025/07/22/all-day-suckers/.

70   "Rebanks describes how farm laborers' traditional skills and relationships withered, their tasks became 'deskilled, boring and dirty' . . . and 'immigrant workers came and went without anyone really knowing their names'": James Rebanks, *English Pastoral: An Inheritance* (Allan Lane, 2020), 139.

71   "'In my father's eyes the work, the land, the cows and the people were all being devalued'": Rebanks, *English Pastoral*, 133.

73   "'The image of nature that became important in the early modern period was that of a disorderly and chaotic realm . . .'": Carolyn Merchant, *The Death of Nature: Women, Ecology and the Scientific Revolution* (Harper & Row, 1980), 127.

73   "Francis Bacon, she writes, 'fashioned a new ethic sanctioning . . .'": Merchant, *The Death of Nature*, 164.

74   "A modern ideology of scarcity 'that sets one neighbor against another in competition for the same goods, so that neighbors . . .'" passim: Walter Brueggemann, interview by Lee C. Camp, podcast interview transcript and recording of a lecture by Brueggemann, posted June 11, 2025, both at https://www.nosmallendeavor.com/walter-brueggemann-the-prophetic-imagination.

7. Honey and the Hive

81   "Goodall describes her lack of an academic background as an asset . . . 'As I had not had an undergraduate science education I didn't realize . . .'": Jane Goodall, *Through a Window: My Thirty Years with the Chimpanzees of Gombe* (Mariner Books, 2000), 32.

82   "Louis Leakey wrote to her, 'Now we must redefine tool, redefine Man, or accept chimpanzees as humans'": Goodall, *Through a Window*, 37.

82   "She wrote: 'Knowing that chimpanzees possess cognitive abilities . . .'": Goodall, *Through a Window*, 262.

83   Lynn Margulis, "On the Origin of Mitosing Cells," *Journal of Theoretical Biology* 14, no. 3 (1967): 255–74.

83   "'Even our own cells were communes'": Martin Brasier, "The Battle of Balliol," in Dorian Sagan, ed., *Lynn Margulis: The Life and Legacy of a Scientific Rebel* (Sciencewriters Books, 2012), 75.

83   "Richard Dawkins . . . declared, 'I greatly admire Lynn Margulis's sheer courage . . .'": quoted as part of a longer passage by Dawkins in John Brockman, "Gaia Is a Tough Bitch," *Edge*, https://www.edge.org/conversation/lynn_margulis-lynn-margulis-1938-2011-gaia-is-a-tough-bitch.

83   "Brasier comments that Margulis and Dawkins, who is now more infamous than famous for his book *The Selfish Gene*, had 'learned

different lessons from the same book of life . . .'": Brasier, "The Battle of Balliol," 77.

84   "Peter Kropotkin summed up Darwin's work as proposing that 'the fittest are not the physically strongest . . .'": in Peter Kropotkin, *Mutual Aid: A Factor of Evolution* (Dover Books, 1902/2006), 2.

84   "Dawkins wrote in *The Selfish Gene*: 'Like successful Chicago gangsters our genes have survived . . .'": Richard Dawkins, *The Selfish Gene: Fortieth Anniversary Edition* (Landmark Science, 2016), 3.

84   "'Algae and host make a miniature ecosystem swimming in the sun'": Lynn Margulis, *Symbiotic Planet: A New Look at Evolution* (Basic Books, 1998), 9–10.

85   "As a pair of scientists put it in 2014, 'Animals, therefore, cannot be regarded as individuals by anatomical criteria, but rather as holobionts . . .'": Seth R. Bordenstein, Kevin R. Theis, "Host Biology in Light of the Microbiome: Ten Principles of Holobionts and Hologenomes," *PLoS Biology* 13, no. 8 (2015): e1002226, https://doi.org/10.1371/journal.pbio.1002226.

85   "The authors write, 'The discovery of symbiosis throughout the animal kingdom is fundamentally transforming the classical conception of an insular individuality . . .'": in Scott F. Gilbert, Jan Sapp, and Albert I. Tauber, "A Symbiotic View of Life: We Have Never Been Individuals," *The Quarterly Review of Biology* 87, no. 4 (2012): 325–41.

85   "Margulis saw it differently, and, after viewing the TV show *Star Trek*, commented acerbically that she 'was struck by its silliness . . .'": Margulis, *Symbiotic Planet*, 104.

86   "Lovelock, she writes in her book *Symbiotic Planet*, 'pointed out that our planetary environment is homeostatic . . .'": Margulis, *Symbiotic Planet*, 117.

88   "As the Nobel Committee put it, [Ostrom] did so 'by conducting field studies on how people in small, local communities manage . . .'": *The Nobel Prize*, Elinor Ostrom, https://www.nobelprize.org/prizes/economic-sciences/2009/ostrom/facts/?sfnsn=scwspmo.

88   Garrett Hardin, "Lifeboat Ethics: The Case Against Helping the Poor," *Psychology Today*, September 1974, https://rintintin.colorado.edu/~vancecd/phil1100/Hardin.pdf.

89   "A few years ago, the *Guardian* asked me to address billionaires as a climate problem . . .": Rebecca Solnit, "Billionaires Are Out of

Touch and Much Too Powerful," *Guardian*, November 20, 2023, https://www.theguardian.com/commentisfree/2023/nov/20/billion-aires-great-carbon-divide-planet-climate-crisis.

90   "'What is usually regarded as "the economy"—wage labor, market exchange of commodities and capitalist enterprise—comprises but a small subset . . .'": Jenny Cameron and J. K. Gibson-Graham, "The Diverse Economies Approach," in Frank Stilwell, David Primrose, and Tim B. Thornton, eds., *Handbook of Alternative Theories of Political Economy* (Edward Elgar Publishing, 2022).

92   "Thomas Seeley, a biologist specializing in bee behavior, who titled one of his books *Honeybee Democracy*, writes, 'Every year, faced with the life-or-death problem of choosing a new home, honeybees stake every-thing on a process . . .'": Thomas Seeley, "The Five Habits of Highly Effective Hives," *Harvard Business Review*, November 11, 2010.

92   "Margulis had used language that approaches a manifesto when she wrote, 'Life is not merely a murderous game . . .'": Lynn Margulis, *Microcosmos* (University of California Press, 1986).

95   "'Ecosystems are so similar to human societies—they're built on re-lationships . . .'": Suzanne Simard, *Finding the Mother Tree* (Alfred A. Knopf, 2021), 189.

96   "The biologist C. Brandon Ogbunu declared, in 2024, 'Modern breakthroughs in biology are producing a picture of life that is increasingly incompatible with authoritarian preferences . . .'": C. Brandon Ogbunu, "In the Authoritarians' New War on Ideas, Biology Might Be Next," *Undark* magazine, October 3, 2024, https://undark.org/2024/10/03/opinion-authoritarian-new-war-on-ideas-biology/.

96   "Simard writes, 'In making the mycorrhizal-network map, I thought we might see a few links. Instead we found a tapestry'": Simard, *Finding the Mother Tree*, 285.

8. The River Widens

101   "Joanna Macy put it, 'Each and every act is understood to have an effect on the larger web of life . . .'": Joanna Macy, *Mutual Causality in Buddhism and General Systems Theory: The Dharma of Natural Systems* (State University of New York Press, 1991), xv, 107.

101   "'The perspective of mutual causality brings to view a world where "everything flows"'": Macy, *Mutual Causality*.

102 Winona LaDuke, "We Are Still Here: The 500 Years Celebration," *Race, Poverty & the Environment* 3, no. 3, Special Issue "Native Nations in 1992: 500 years of Cultural Survival" (Fall 1992): 3, 20–21, https://www.jstor.org/stable/i40074959.

105 "Charles C. Mann writes, 'As late as 1987 *American History: A Survey . . .*'": Charles C. Mann, "1491," *Atlantic*, March 2002.

108 "[Benjamin Hedin and Nick Estes] note that the 1932 book of interviews known as *Black Elk Speaks . . .*": Benjamin Hedin and Nick Estes, "The Siege of Wounded Knee Was Not an Ending but a Beginning," *New Yorker*, May 26, 2023.

110 "'We're the ancestors of tomorrow,' said Madonna Thunder Hawk": see epigraph, above.

113 "While receiving the 2025 Goldman award, Murayari said that the spirits that reside in the waters . . .": Goldman Environmental Foundation, "Mari Luz Canaquiri Murayari," speech, 2025, https://www.goldmanprize.org/recipient/mari-luz-canaquiri-murayari/.

114 "In the report Carr sent me, by the Intergovernmental Science-Policy Platform on Biodiversity and Ecosystem Services . . .": IPBES, *Summary for Policymakers of the Thematic Assessment Report on the Underlying Causes of Biodiversity Loss and the Determinants of Transformative Change and Options for Achieving the 2050 Vision for Biodiversity* (2024), https://www.ipbes.net/transformative-change-assessment.

115 "The Indigenous scholar Natalie Avalos writes, 'In the last few years, Indigenous peoples have reemerged as a critical voice . . .'": Natalie Avalos, "Indigenous Stewardship and the Death Rattle of White Supremacy," *Political Theology*, June 25, 2020, https://politicaltheology.com/indigenous-stewardship-and-the-death-rattle-of-white-supremacy/.

116 "We find ourselves at an extraordinary moment, when after years of attempted erasure . . .": Robin Wall Kimmerer, quoted in "Celebrating the Decade-Long Impact of *Braiding Sweetgrass*," Milkweed, September 20, 2023, https://milkweed.org/blog/celebrating-the-decade-long-impact-of-braiding-sweetgrass.

116 "David Graeber and archeologist David Wengrow argue that . . .": David Graeber and David Wengrow, "In the Considered Opinion of the Montagnais-Naskapi," in *The Dawn of Everything: A New History of Humanity* (Farrar, Straus, and Giroux, 2021), 40–41.

118 "Robin Wall Kimmerer writes that Indigenous language 'challenges the fundamental tenets of Western thinking . . .'": Robin Wall Kimmerer, "Speaking of Nature: Finding Language That Affirms Our Kinship with the World," *Orion*, June 12, 2017.

119 "Zadie Smith said, in a recent interview, 'It's something that I dreamed about all my life . . .'": Zadie Smith, interview by Ezra Klein, *New York Times*, September 17, 2024.

9. Otherwise

121 "Jim Harrison wrote, 'I decided we were born to be moving water not ice'": Jim Harrison, "River 1" (poem), in *Songs of Unreason* (Copper Canyon Press, 2011), 67.

121 "John Dupré and Daniel J. Nicholson write, 'The right way to understand the living world at all levels is as a hierarchy of processes . . .'": John Dupré and Daniel J. Nicholson, eds., *Everything Flows: Towards a Processual Philosophy of Biology* (Oxford University Press, 2018), https://academic.oup.com/book/27525/chapter/197490752.

124 "Mike Davis drew hope from that past he lived through and participated in, saying to an interviewer not long before his death, in 2022, 'This seems an age of catastrophe, but it's also an age equipped . . .'": Dana Goodyear, "Mike Davis in the Age of Catastrophe," *New Yorker*, April 24, 2020.

124 "As David Graeber reminded us, 'The ultimate hidden truth of the world . . .'": David Graeber, *The Utopia of Rules: On Technology, Stupidity and the Secret Joys of Bureaucracy* (Melville House, 2015), online at https://theanarchistlibrary.org/library/david-graeber-the-utopia-of-rules.

124 "Fredric Jameson is supposed to have said, 'It's easier to imagine the end of the world than the end of capitalism'": the quote is sometimes said to be something he quoted someone else saying or that someone else actually said.

125 "Deb Haaland said, of her Laguna Pueblo heritage, 'When I was a child, my mom didn't teach us Keres . . .'": Deb Haaland, Facebook, August 23, 2024, https://www.facebook.com/SecretaryDebHaaland/posts/when-i-was-a-child-my-mom-didnt-teach-us-keres-our-native-language-her-years-of-/494790053153361/.

125 "Pete Buttigieg, who, with his husband Chasten, adopted twins a few years ago, said, 'The existence of my family is just one example of something that was literally impossible . . .'": Pete Buttigieg, speech, Democratic National Convention, August 21, 2024, posted by Ian Schwartz at Real Clear Politics, https://www.realclearpolitics.com/video/2024/08/21/ buttigieg_vance_is_that_guy_who_thinks_if_you_dont_live_the_life_ he_has_in_mind_for_you_then_you_dont_count.html.

125 "Cleve Jones, who was born in 1954 and wrote in his memoir, 'I was born into the last generation of homosexual people who grew up not knowing . . .'": Cleve Jones, *When We Rise: My Life in the Movement* (Hachette, 2016), 1.

128 "[Anand Giridharadas] wrote, 'I see then that this is both a very dark time and, potentially, a very bright time . . .'": see Giridharadas, epigraph, above.

128 "Giridharadas went on, 'We are living through a revolt against the future . . .'": see Giridharadas, epigraph, above.

128 "Arundhati Roy had put it another way in her address to the World Social Forum in 2003: 'Another world is not only possible . . .'": Arundhati Roy, *Nation*, February 20, 2003, from a speech at the World Social Forum, Porto Alegre, Brazil, January 20, 2003, https:// www.thenation.com/article/archive/confronting-empire/.

130 "[Joanna Macy] had said in an interview, 'There's a song that wants to sing itself through us . . .'": Joanna Macy, interview by Krista Tippet, *On Being*, September 16, 2010, https://onbeing.org/programs/joanna-macy-a-wild-love-for-the-world.

131 "'We are creating a world we have never seen,' wrote adrienne maree brown in *Emergent Strategy*": adrienne maree brown, *Emergent Strategy* (AK Press, 2017), 163.

About the Author

REBECCA SOLNIT is the author of more than twenty books, including *Orwell's Roses*, *Hope in the Dark*, *Men Explain Things to Me*, *A Paradise Built in Hell: The Extraordinary Communities That Arise in Disaster*, and *A Field Guide to Getting Lost*. A longtime climate and human rights activist, she serves on the boards of the climate groups Oil Change International and Third Act. Her newsletter of essays and analyses can be found at meditationsinanemergency.com.

About Haymarket Books

Haymarket Books is a radical, independent, nonprofit book publisher based in Chicago. Our mission is to publish books that contribute to struggles for social and economic justice. We strive to make our books a vibrant and organic part of social movements and the education and development of a critical, engaged, and internationalist left.

We take inspiration and courage from our namesakes, the Haymarket Martyrs, who gave their lives fighting for a better world. Their 1886 struggle for the eight-hour day—which gave us May Day, the international workers' holiday—reminds workers around the world that ordinary people can organize and struggle for their own liberation. These struggles—against oppression, exploitation, environmental devastation, and war—continue today across the globe.

Since our founding in 2001, Haymarket has published more than nine hundred titles. Radically independent, we seek to drive a wedge into the risk-averse world of corporate book publishing. Our authors include Angela Y. Davis, Arundhati Roy, Keeanga-Yamahtta Taylor, Eve Ewing, Aja Monet, Mariame Kaba, Naomi Klein, Rebecca Solnit, Olúfẹ́mi O. Táíwò, Mohammed El-Kurd, José Olivarez, Noam Chomsky, Winona LaDuke, Robyn Maynard, Leanne Betasamosake Simpson, Howard Zinn, Mike Davis, Marc Lamont Hill, Dave Zirin, Astra Taylor, and Amy Goodman, among many other leading writers of our time. We are also the trade publishers of the acclaimed Historical Materialism Book Series.

Haymarket also manages a vibrant community organizing and event space in Chicago, Haymarket House, the popular Haymarket Books Live event series and podcast, and the annual Socialism Conference.